EVERY GOOD THING

An Introduction to the Material World
and the Common Good for Christians

EVERY GOOD THING

An Introduction to the Material World
and the Common Good for Christians

David W. Jones

Every Good Thing:
An Introduction to the Material World
and the Common Good for Christians

Copyright 2016 David W. Jones

Lexham Press, 1313 Commercial St., Bellingham, WA 98225
LexhamPress.com

Print ISBN 9781577997016
Digital ISBN 9781577997023

Lexham Editorial: Rebecca Brant, Abigail Stocker
Cover Design: Max Morin
Typesetting: ProjectLuz.com

For Dawn

"She rises before daylight ...
and her lamp does not go out by night."
—Proverbs 31:15, 18

TABLE OF CONTENTS

would like to thank many people for making this book possible. First, I would like to thank the administration of Southeastern Baptist Theological Seminary for giving me time to write this book. I would also like to thank the Kern Family Foundation for their generous grant, which helped to finance this project. I would be remiss if I didn't thank the many editors and proofreaders who painstakingly helped to make this volume readable—these include Dawn Jones, Billie Goodenough, Devin Maddox, and others (of course, any errors you find are my own). I would also like to thank the many students who, through their questions and dialogue over the years, have unknowingly helped to shape the content of this book.

This is a little book on a big topic: the material world. Where do we start? Let me begin with some personal background.

When I was 12 years old, I began working as a day laborer on an apple farm. Every weekday after school and all day on Saturdays, I went to work on the farm. I was paid minimum wage for carrying out various tasks: harvesting apples, picking strawberries, selling pumpkins, preparing fields for planting, pulling weeds, staffing the farmer's market, and various other farm-related chores. It was hard work, but good work.

While my career path has taken me out of agriculture and into academia, I am so thankful for those early years of working on the farm. It was in those rural fields that I developed a biblical work ethic and began to ask some of the questions that would help to determine my life's trajectory.

Early on, for example, I experienced the satisfaction that comes from a hard day's labor, and I quickly learned about the need (of people and land) for regular rest, too. On the farm I was affected by the revelation and wonder that comes from being in constant contact with the created order, cut off from the hustle and drone of culture. My farm job also exposed me to real poverty for the first time since many of my colaborers were migrant workers who lived communally in relative squalor. In contrast, my work also prompted me to begin asking questions about wealth: To my 12-year-old self, earning $3.35/hour made me feel rich, like I would if I were making $1,000/hour today.

These types of issues began to interest me when I was a boy—and they ought to interest all of us, for they are inescapable facts of the world in which we live and work. Moreover, Scripture addresses all these topics—wealth and poverty, work and rest, creation and stewardship. As I began to walk with God as a young man, I wanted to know what the Bible had to say about issues related to the material realm.

Although some Christians seem to live a compartmentalized life in which the gospel has only spiritual value, I became convinced early in my Christian walk (and am even more so today) that the gospel relates to all areas of life. Indeed, Christianity is a worldview and life-view that is all-encompassing. The gospel applies to every area of human existence—be it physical, emotional, or spiritual. This book explores some thoughts on this topic.

Here's how the discussion unfolds over the following pages. Chapter 1 explores some foundational issues related to the material world and defines some of the fundamental terms and concepts that we'll use throughout the book. We'll also look at the example of Jesus in regard to his incarnation in and interaction with the world.

Chapter 2 focuses on work and vocation. We'll construct a biblical theology of work by looking at some common misconceptions about work, the divinely designed foundations of work, the distortion of work, and the restoration of work brought about by the gospel. We'll also examine the value of work and the concept of vocation. As we'll see, God designed people to work, and we all have specific vocations to fulfill.

Chapter 3 complements the preceding discussion with a focus on rest and Sabbath. We'll rely on the fourth commandment—the moral law addressing the Sabbath—as our guide to this topic. We'll also review some of the Old Testament civil laws that relate to stewardship and economics since the Sabbath is the moral basis for many of the finance-related laws in the Bible.

In chapter 4 our exploration turns to issues related specifically to wealth and poverty, including giving (with a discussion of tithing), the causes of poverty, various strategies for ministering to the poor, and the idea of social justice. We'll also develop a biblical theology of wealth and poverty.

Finally, in chapter 5, we'll wrap up our study of the material world by looking at creation and stewardship. We'll take a bird's-eye view of the created order with the goal of better understanding the realm in which we work and rest, enjoy wealth and endure poverty. In this chapter we'll also study some basic principles related to the care of creation, assess the effects of sin on the present world, and briefly review the hope of a new heaven and a new earth.

CHAPTER 1

Fundamentals and Foundations

I f we are being honest, many of us would admit we have a hard time understanding how Christianity relates to our lives Monday through Saturday. Sure, we know we're supposed to apply the simple takeaways from each Sunday's sermon—keep the Ten Commandments and "be like Jesus." But it's challenging for most of us to bridge the gap between seeing Christianity as a Sunday-only phenomenon (or an eternal-life insurance policy) and seeing how faith and the Bible relate to all of life. This is especially true when it comes to living in the material world.

The material world: What are we as Christians to think of it? How does God call us to live in it? Let's start by defining what we mean by "material world" so that we're all on the same page. Put most simply, the material world is the world in which we live. We could also use the term "material realm" or, in some cases, "created realm" or "created order." This world involves not only our physical surroundings, but also how we conduct ourselves as believers in the context of our families, workplaces, and communities, both local and global.

With that understanding, let's move on to explore believers' various perceptions of the material world. Many Christians seem to think the material realm is evil—after all, we're supposed to focus on the spiritual realm, right? Many define Christianity as making sure people are born again, filled with the Holy Spirit, and headed for an eternal spiritual existence before God in heaven. Some perceive the material world as the realm of sin, temptation, greed, and principalities and powers of darkness. These believers may wonder why Christians should be concerned about the material world and its related issues. True, most of us embrace the vague idea that we are supposed to care for poor people (Jesus did) and to give to our churches (the bills need to be paid), and no one wants to be thought of as lazy. Yet, is there more to living in the material world as Christians?

This little book aims to show that as Christians we *must* be concerned with the material world, both for our own good and for the good of our neighbors. Indeed, biblically speaking, the material here-and-now is just as important as the sweet by-and-by. God cares about the created realm, and he cares about the way we live. Scripture speaks about issues such as wealth and poverty, work and rest, economics and finance, and we will cover some of its teachings on these topics. The goal of this work, then, is to help you, as a follower of Jesus Christ, better understand how to live in the material world for the common good.

The Material World

With so little teaching in Christian circles about living in the material world, we may wonder why we should care about it at all. When was the last time you heard a good sermon on wealth, work, or vocation, for example? Have you read a good Christian book recently on ministering to the poor, keeping the Sabbath, or participating in mercy ministries? Probably not, if you're like most believers. When Christians do teach about the material world, we tend to get it wrong in one extreme or the other—from a fundamentalist mentality of "it's all going to burn up one day anyway" to the prosperity gospel and its false promises of health, wealth, and happiness for a small, recurring monthly donation.

Despite the relative lack or distortion of gospel-centric teaching about the created realm, Christians should care about material issues for a number of reasons. First and foremost is that the Bible is filled with teachings related to the material world. We're familiar with many such passages: "For the love of money is a root of all kinds of evils" (1 Tim 6:10); "If anyone is not willing to work, let him not eat" (2 Thess 3:10); and "For you always have the poor with you" (Matt 26:11). And there are scores of lesser-known passages that address everything from saving and lending to social justice and financial ethics. When considered in total, the Bible is a surprisingly material-oriented, earthy book.

Of course, the material world is where we live. We ought to be concerned with how we interact, as believers, with our families, workplaces, and communities. Faith without real-life value is useless. If Christianity is a legitimate world- and life-view, we ought to expect that it will speak to material issues. We ought to desire to know what the Bible says about such things—and we need to get it right in practice. Those who say they want to be saved so that they can live as they please clearly don't understand the offer or extent of the gospel.

The Bible is clear that Jesus cared about the material world. His example—which we will look at shortly—and message was not one of detachment from the physical realm, but one of involvement. Indeed, the incarnation itself proves this. Have you ever noticed the recurring material, economic, and stewardship-oriented themes in Jesus' teachings—let alone the ease with which he moved between the rich and the poor? For instance, the Gospel narratives reveal Jesus freely interacting with people of all economic statuses. In addition, Christ spoke in his parables about workers, owners, stewards, creditors, debtors, pearls, coins, fish, talents, minas, investing, wealth, poverty—the list goes on. Very earthy stuff. It's hard to imagine that someone could really have the mind of Christ without being interested in the material world with which Jesus was so familiar and concerned.

We also have a very practical reason to investigate what the Bible says about material things: Our perspective on this issue will affect our own flourishing. As with all of God's revelation in Scripture, there is a certain practicality that comes with knowledge of content and obedience to commands. We can call this "human flourishing" or "the common good." Since God does not randomly give humanity directives but rather created us to do what he tells us to do, getting it right or wrong in regard to the created order will affect our contentment (from a personal perspective), our discipleship (from the church's perspective), and even our witness (from the lost world's perspective).

So, if the Bible speaks both directly and indirectly about material issues, if the material world is where we presently live, if Jesus' life and ministry demonstrate his concern with the created realm, and if we have a practical vested interest in what God reveals to us in the Bible, then the question is not why *should* we care about the material world, but why *don't* we care about it? Knowing what the Bible says about money, economics, stewardship, work, and the like is not just an option for Christians; it's an opportunity to be Christ-like, to flourish, and to be relevant to those around us.

Economics and Stewardship

Once we realize that the gospel affects the created order, we are naturally going to have questions: Is it more spiritual to be poor? Is it okay to be wealthy? Will I become rich if I serve God? How do we justify our wealth when so many are in need around the world? How do we care for the poor? How much money should I give to my church? Such questions are limitless, and the questions change with time and culture. While no one book could possibly answer all such questions, I hope to address some foundational themes that will enable you to live in the material world for the common good.

You can admit it: If this book was titled *Economic Theory and Christian Living* or *The Bible and Stewardship*, you probably wouldn't be reading it, right? I wouldn't either. Economics and stewardship sound boring. However, since this book is about living in the material realm, it will draw upon and include topics and concepts related to economics and stewardship—such as the transfer of material goods through commerce and monetary exchange, or labor and compensation in the workplace. But don't put the book down just yet! I hope to show you that these ideas are not boring.

When I say "economics" I am not talking about the stock market or your 401(k) plan at work—at least not directly. The term "economy" comes from an ancient Greek word that means "the law of the house." So when we speak about economics, we're really talking about housekeeping—ordering and arranging the material things in the place where we live. If we view life through a wide-angle lens, we could say that the world is the house in which we live, and our interaction with other people and the material stuff of the world involves or is an act of economics. Of course, it's a lot easier to say you're interested in knowing what the Bible says about living in the material world than it is to say you want to know about biblical economics. But either way, we are talking about the same thing. It's all housekeeping.

"Stewardship" is a very similar concept. I know—when you hear the term "stewardship" you think about those too-frequent, guilt-inducing sermons. Giving money to your church can be a form of stewardship (or a form of legalism!), and it certainly is important, but it doesn't embody the entirety of the concept. The modern term "steward" comes from the Old English word *stigweard*, which means "housekeeper." Stewardship, then, involves taking care of someone else's stuff—namely, the homeowner's material possessions. So, to return to our wide-angle lens, we can say that stewardship is the faithful management of God's resources in God's world to achieve God's objectives.

When we talk about living in the material world, then, we're actually having a discussion about economics and stewardship. We're talking about the efficient use of God's resources—neither wasting nor hoarding—as we live and interact with others. Indeed, Jesus appealed to just living— or being a good steward—in the parable of the Talents (see Matt 25:14-30). Conversely, Christ speaks about being a poor steward and interacting with others unjustly in the parable of the Tenants (although that is not the main theme; see Mark 12:1-11). Since Jesus talked about these things, we know that to live in the material world for the common good, we need to wisely handle the resources that God has entrusted to us, realizing he is ultimately the owner of the vineyard.

Material Wealth and Poverty

When we talk about living in the material world for the common good, the themes of wealth and poverty often arise. Of course, this is quite natural, for wealth and poverty are the concepts we use to measure the presence or absence of material goods. Although we'll talk in greater depth about wealth and poverty later (see chapter 4), it will be helpful to define these two concepts as we begin this discussion about the material world. But as we'll see, defining "wealth" and "poverty" might not be as easy as we might think.

What is wealth? What is poverty? How do we determine if we are rich or poor? Although these may seem like easy questions, the more thought we give to them, the harder they are to answer in an objective manner. Material wealth and poverty are typically determined within a certain context, relative to our immediate or cultural proximity and era. We're not saying that everyone gets to make up their own definitions of wealth and poverty; rather, we're saying that how we measure wealth and poverty is affected by when and where we live.

For example, by almost every conceivable material measurement, the average person living at the government-defined poverty level in the United States in the 21st century has a better (that is, more wealthy) life than the vast majority of individuals who lived in the first century. This is not because there are more or fewer wealthy or poor people living in either time period; it's because we're comparing different eras. So, while a dictionary may define wealth as the presence of material abundance and affluence and poverty as having few or no material possessions, it's important to understand that these concepts are, necessarily, relative measurements.

Of course, given a choice, most people would choose wealth over poverty, regardless of how the status is measured. I know I would. Yet it's interesting to note that the Bible describes each of these conditions as both a blessing and a curse. Let's consider wealth first. Moses taught Israel,

"Remember the LORD your God, for it is he who gives you power to get wealth" (Deut 8:18). If God enables us to attain wealth, it must be a blessing. Scripture is full of examples of godly rich people—such as the patriarchs, Job, David, Solomon, and Joseph of Arimathea, among others. Since God is the source of wealth, and given the examples in Scripture of rich individuals who love God, it would seem honorable to desire wealth, if not to view wealth as a mark of godliness.

Yet the Bible's teachings on wealth are not always quite so positive. For instance, in an often-cited verse, Jesus said, "It is easier for a camel to go through the eye of a needle than for a rich person to enter the kingdom of God" (Matt 19:24). Similarly, in the parable of the Sower, Christ taught that the cares of this world, including wealth, will prevent some people from entering heaven (see Matt 13:7, 22). The Bible offers many examples of the ungodly rich: the apostate kings of Israel and Judah; Nabal; and several wealthy individuals who appear in Jesus' ministry, including the rich young man (Matt 19:16–26) and the rich man in the Lazarus parable (Luke 16:19–31)—both of whom chose wealth over a right relationship with God. Perhaps having wealth, then, is not as desirable as we first thought.

Poverty is an equally difficult concept to pin down in Scripture. While few modern Christians in Western culture would volunteer for a life of poverty, this is apparently exactly what Jesus' disciples did, as they willingly "left everything and followed [Jesus]" (Matt 19:27). Jesus also taught, "Blessed are you who are poor, for yours is the kingdom of God" (Luke 6:20). We might be tempted to think Jesus is speaking only of spiritual poverty here, as Matthew records Jesus' similar teaching on a different occasion about "the poor in spirit" (Matt 5:3). However, in light of Luke's parallel woe (see Luke 6:24), Jesus is clearly teaching about the materially poor in Luke 6:20—again saying they are blessed. Of course, there are biblical examples of godly poor people throughout the Bible, including Jesus himself (who had no place to lay his head), Lazarus the beggar (who died and went to heaven), and the apostles (who, we just noted, left everything to follow Jesus).

However, poverty is not always—or even usually—presented as a blessing or a mark of spiritual maturity in Scripture. For example, the proverbs repeatedly warn about and teach that poverty can be the result of personal sin. To cite a few passages, Proverbs 23:21 warns, "The drunkard and the glutton will come to poverty, and slumber will clothe them with rags," and Proverbs 28:19 teaches, "Whoever works his land will have plenty of bread, but he who follows worthless pursuits will have plenty of poverty." Furthermore, God often identifies poverty as accompanying judgment (see Deut 28:30-42; Jer 5:17-19; Mic 6:13-16). So, then, poverty may not always be a preferential option for Christians.

We cannot identify either status as being inherently favorable or unfavorable in Scripture. Discussions about wealth and poverty that begin with the assumption that either is always evil (or a blessing) will inevitably come to wrong conclusions. In the ensuing discussion, we'll see that the Bible has more to say about how we arrive at and handle our material status than it does about the inherent morality of wealth or poverty. We have only to remember: Paul taught that it is the love of money, not money itself, that is evil (see 1 Tim 6:10). Similarly, Jesus' teachings on wealth and poverty seem to focus more on what's in our heart than what's in our hands.

Spiritual Wealth and Poverty

As we examine what it means to live in the material realm, we would be negligent if we didn't note that when the Bible talks about wealth and poverty, the teaching is not always material in nature. Indeed, when the authors of Scripture speak about being rich or poor, they are sometimes speaking spiritually. This is an important observation because if we read a spiritual teaching in the Bible as if it were material or vice versa, we may find our interpretation of a given passage to be beyond the bounds of orthodoxy. Let's investigate this further.

Consider the following statement from Paul to the Corinthian church: "For you know the grace of our Lord Jesus Christ, that though he was rich, yet for your sake he became poor, so that you by his poverty might become rich" (2 Cor 8:9). Was Paul teaching that we can expect to be materially wealthy if we love Jesus? Advocates of the prosperity gospel certainly think so. Yet this has not been the practical experience of the majority of Christians, nor is it the experience of most Christians who live in the non-Western world. So is Paul writing about material or spiritual wealth and poverty in this passage?

Cues like personal experience, context, and Paul's teachings elsewhere in his letters can help us understand that Paul is writing about spiritual wealth and poverty in this passage. Any responsible, orthodox Bible commentary should prove this point. Yet this verse raises two important questions. First, when a passage mentions wealth and poverty, how do we know if it is speaking materially or spiritually (if we don't have a commentary handy)? Second, is there a relationship between material wealth/poverty and spiritual wealth/poverty? I believe that understanding how to answer this second question can guide us as we seek to answer the first.

Connecting Material and Spiritual States

Logically speaking, there are four different ways in which material wealth/poverty and spiritual wealth/poverty can be connected. To claim that any one of these possible arrangements is fixed, I believe, is erroneous. Here's a summary of the possible arrangements:

- First, the belief that material wealth is a sign of spiritual wealth is the aforementioned error known as the prosperity gospel.

- Second, to claim that material poverty is a sure sign of spiritual poverty is to commit the error of Job's friends.

- Third, the belief that material wealth is always a sign of spiritual poverty is the error of materialism (an earlier generation called this the sin of cupidity).

- Fourth, the idea that material poverty is a sign of spiritual wealth is the error of monasticism.

If you're struggling to grasp these four relationships, reread this paragraph a few times. We'll unpack some of the details below.

As stated above, I believe it is erroneous to claim that any one of the four possible connections mentioned above contains a fixed or causal relationship. Yet, over time, each of these arrangements has proven attractive to certain groups of believers (or, at least, to groups who claim to be Christian) because each relationship presents a *possible* but not a *fixed* connection. Each of these arrangements between material wealth/poverty and spiritual wealth/poverty has a grain of truth to it; however, it may be no more than a grain. Let's look at these relationships more closely, as we identify erroneous understandings as well as the possible connection between these material and spiritual statuses.

The prosperity gospel claims that material wealth is a sign of spiritual wealth. In other words, preachers of this false gospel claim that mature faith results in material abundance. While this is an error (indeed, a heresy), it is true that material wealth can be connected to spiritual wealth. For example, as we mature spiritually, we often develop moral character traits—including industry, honesty, diligence, punctuality—which can lead to an increase in material wealth. As Solomon taught, "The hand of the diligent makes rich. ... The plans of the diligent lead surely to abundance" (Prov 10:4; 21:5). So material wealth and spiritual wealth can be related, but this is not always the case.

Job's friends made the inaccurate claim that Job's material poverty was the direct result of some unconfessed sin arising from his spiritual poverty. Of course, we know this claim was not true, since God declared as much in Job 42:7-8 (look it up!). Yet there is truth to the notion that material poverty can be connected to spiritual poverty. As we explored earlier, the teaching that spiritual poverty leads to material poverty is a recurring theme in the Bible, especially in the book of Proverbs. For example, "A slack hand causes poverty. ... Mere talk tends only to poverty. ... Love not sleep, lest you come to poverty. ... He who follows worthless pursuits will have plenty of poverty" (Prov 10:4; 14:23; 20:13; 28:19). Material poverty, then, can be connected to spiritual poverty, but this is not always the case. There are other causes of material poverty, including personal choice.

Materialism—a preoccupation with the material world to the neglect of spiritual things—is a problem in many affluent Western countries (we'll discuss this more in chapter 5). While it's an error to believe that material wealth is always a sign of spiritual poverty, it is nevertheless true that many rich individuals live lives characterized by sin. Scripture repeatedly warns us about putting the love of money above the love of God and gives negative examples of those who have done so (see Matt 6:19-20; Luke 12:13-21). Yet, in light of the positive examples and teachings about wealth in the Bible, it seems clear that material wealth and spiritual poverty are not always connected.

Finally, the idea that material poverty is a sign of spiritual wealth is the error of monasticism. Think of monks and nuns who have taken a vow of poverty and who live with few material possessions in an attempt to please God. True, these monks and nuns may be spiritually mature, yet they may be spiritually poor if they're trying to earn their salvation through good works. While common sense may demonstrate that material poverty and spiritual wealth are not always related, it is nevertheless true that sometimes "God [chooses] those who are poor in the world to be rich in faith and heirs of the kingdom" (Jas 2:5). Again, we see a possible connection between these material and spiritual statuses, but not a fixed, causal relationship.

So it seems that two conclusions are in order. First, the Bible speaks of both material wealth and poverty and spiritual wealth and poverty. In reading any given passage, it's important that we discern if the text is speaking materially or spiritually. Second, it is an error to believe that material wealth/poverty and spiritual wealth/poverty are connected in a fixed manner. Often these statuses are connected, but the relationship is not always (or even usually) causal.

The Example of Jesus

As we've covered some foundational topics in this opening chapter, one question that we have yet to ask is, "What would Jesus do?" Perhaps a better question would be, "What *did* Jesus do?" What was the example of our Savior as he lived in the material world, as he interacted with the things and people who fill it? Certainly, we need to follow the example of Jesus. As Christians (literally, "little Christs"), we ought to be interested in both what Jesus said and what he did. However, when it comes to living in the material world and being Christ-like, interpreting the biblical example of Jesus can be challenging. This is not because Jesus was inconsistent in his example; it is because Christ's interaction with the material world was so wide ranging.

In reading the Gospels, it is possible to read with a focus on Jesus' poverty. There is a sense in which Christ's incarnation itself was an impoverishing act. Indeed, in order to take on human flesh and dwell among sinful people and the filth of this world, Jesus had to set aside the wealth of heaven. This was Paul's teaching in Philippians 2:7, where he wrote that Jesus "emptied himself [of his privileges], by taking the form of a servant, being born in the likeness of men." This same teaching is the essence of the previously cited verse, "For you know the grace of our Lord Jesus Christ, that though he was rich, yet for your sake he became poor, so that you by his poverty might become rich" (2 Cor 8:9).

We can also see the level of poverty that Jesus experienced by looking at the material state of his family. Most people are familiar with the details of Christ's birth since they are recounted and celebrated every Christmas. Jesus' nativity story includes being born in a foreign city (presumably without family and friends), being placed in a manger (literally a feed trough), and being visited by shepherds—strangers who were considered by most people to be the outcasts of society (see Luke 2:7).

In describing Jesus' circumcision, Luke reports that Mary and Joseph offered two pigeons as a temple sacrifice for Mary's purification (see Luke 2:22-24). Leviticus 12:7-8 explains that the usual sacrifice at the time of circumcision was to be a lamb, but if the birth mother could not "afford a lamb, then she shall take two turtledoves or two pigeons, one for a burnt offering and the other for a sin offering. And the priest shall make atonement for her, and she shall be clean" (Lev 12:8). Apparently, then, Jesus' parents were too poor to offer the customary lamb.

It seems clear, then, that Jesus was born into a family that was part of the lower economic class. We see this material status has not changed 30 years later, during Jesus' earthly ministry. We've already cited a number of Jesus' well-known teachings about wealth and poverty at this time. We should note, too, Jesus' comments on his own economic status, such as when he said, "Foxes have holes, and birds of the air have nests, but the Son of Man has nowhere to lay his head" (Matt 8:20). The Gospel narratives bear out this testimony.

It appears that Christ had very little by way of material possessions during his ministry. Consider the following: Jesus preached from borrowed boats, multiplied borrowed food, rode on a borrowed colt, and was buried in a borrowed tomb. In fact, most of Jesus' material needs, as well as those of his disciples, were apparently met by donations from a group of devoted women who accompanied him. In his Gospel, Luke refers to "Mary, called Magdalene, from whom seven demons had gone out, and Joanna, the wife of Chuza, Herod's household manager, and Susanna, and many others, who provided for [Jesus and his disciples] out of their means" (Luke 8:2-3; see also Mark 15:40-41).

If this description could be taken as a comprehensive summary of how Jesus lived in the material world during his incarnation, we could conclude that his example was one of poverty and that our lives should likewise aim toward poverty. However, it is also possible to read the Gospels with a focus on Jesus' wealth.

As we just noted, the economic status of Jesus' family at the time of his birth was clearly one of poverty or near-poverty. Yet, three years later when the magi visited Christ, bringing extremely costly gifts, Jesus' family was situated in a house, which indicates a probable increase in Mary and Joseph's economic status (see Matt 2:11). Later, in Luke 2:41-51, the Gospel writer reports that Mary and Joseph had enough financial stability to travel as a family to Jerusalem to celebrate the Passover feast—a journey that was only required of adult males, not entire families (see Exod 23:17).

The Bible does not explain details about the improved financial status of Jesus' family; however, it is likely that over time they became part of what we would identify as the economic middle class. Historians tell us Nazareth was a prosperous town, especially for tradesmen, since it was located near the city of Sepphoris, a luxurious Roman vacation destination that was under constant construction. We can surmise that Joseph, being a carpenter (Matt 13:55), would have benefited from this opportunity for steady employment. Evidently, Jesus eventually took up his father's trade, since he was later known as "the carpenter" (Mark 6:3).

The Bible also reports that Jesus ministered to and identified with many wealthy and powerful individuals, including

Joseph of Arimathea, Nicodemus, Zacchaeus, Levi, and certain unnamed Pharisees. Luke's Gospel especially highlights Jesus' enjoyment of food, his acceptance of costly gifts, and his keeping company with the wealthy. For example, Luke records Jesus' attendance at parties and his dining with wealthy individuals (see Luke 5:29–32; 7:36–39; 11:37; 14:1–2). Some of these same themes appear in the Gospel of John, which reports Christ's first miracle to have occurred at a wedding celebration and later notes Jesus' acceptance of a gift of costly, luxurious perfume from Mary (see John 2:1–11; 12:1–3). Note Jesus' testimony regarding himself: "The Son of Man came eating and drinking" (Matt 11:19).

Based on the example of Jesus' life, what are we to conclude about living in the material world? During his lifetime, Jesus experienced a range of economic statuses. He would have experienced relative poverty at his birth, a first-century middle-class upbringing prior to embarking on his ministry, and then voluntary poverty during his ministry. It is telling to note that Christ never condemned wealth or poverty itself; rather, he confronted sins that often led to wealth or poverty—sins including greed, pride, laziness, injustice, and theft, among others. Moreover, it is clear that Jesus was comfortable with and proficient at interacting with both rich and poor.

By way of application, then, it seems that to be Christlike, we need to learn to be content in our own material circumstances, whatever they may be (Phil 4:11). Seeking to change our financial status, whether from poverty to wealth or from wealth to poverty, seems permissible, as long as our motives are godly. Furthermore, it is Christ-like to confront sins that result in an unjust material state, whether it be poverty or wealth. Cultivating the ability to talk with the poor and the rich alike will be a helpful skill as we seek to reach the world with the gospel of Christ.

Heading Forward

We covered a lot of ground in this opening chapter as we looked at some of the foundational issues related to living in the material world. After discussing how our exploration relates to economics and stewardship, we noted that neither wealth nor poverty is an inherently favored status in Scripture. Next, we investigated the relationship between material wealth/poverty and spiritual wealth/poverty. We concluded that while there is often a connection between the material and spiritual realm, any relationship that does exist is not necessarily fixed or causal. Finally, we looked at the example of Jesus, which included both material wealth and poverty.

At this point, you can understand the importance of knowing what the Bible says about living in the material world, and you have an initial grasp of some of the terminology and concepts that we'll appeal to as we seek to explore this issue in more detail. The first topic we'll investigate is the biblical teaching on work and vocation.

Summary

- Many Christians don't know how to think about the material world, or they view the created order in a surprisingly unbiblical manner.

- Jesus' example was not one of detachment from the physical realm, but one of involvement.

- The concepts of wealth and poverty are relative concepts in their measurement, and Scripture does not favor either material status.

- Material wealth/poverty and spiritual wealth/poverty are connected in a noncausal manner.

- During his incarnation, Jesus experienced both material wealth and material poverty while never condemning either status.

Action Points

- What is a biblical definition of the material world?

- Did Jesus care more about the material world or the spiritual world?

- What do material wealth and poverty have to do with spiritual wealth and poverty?

CHAPTER 2

Work and Vocation

Work: Few of us are fond of the concept. The terms "work" and "labor" don't usually prompt us to smile. Conversely, everyone likes the weekend. TGIF, right? So why do we like the weekend? Because we don't have to go to work! And when the alarm goes off on Monday morning, we wish it were still the weekend. But is this perspective biblical? Is it inherently satisfying? Might there be some redeeming quality to work? Let's take a closer look.

Bible scholars tell us the concept of work is mentioned, explicitly or implicitly, more than 800 times in Scripture. I have not attempted to track down and catalog all of these references, but this statistic seems reasonable to me. Consider just a few of the examples and general teachings on work that stand out as you read through the Bible. For example, as we mentioned in the previous chapter, Jesus was the son of a carpenter—a blue-collar tradesman—and Jesus eventually became a tradesman himself (see Matt 13:55; Mark 6:3). For some people, this can be a challenging characterization of Christ. Many prefer to think of Jesus with a halo, like in a medieval painting. Indeed, to some people it seems irreligious to think of Jesus covered in sweat and sawdust, dealing with demanding customers, exhausted at the end of a day's labor. Yet this is the Jesus of the Bible.

Paul, too, was a manual laborer—a tentmaker (see Acts 18:3; 20:34). Not only was Paul a tradesman, but also he appealed to his own labor as an example for the church, writing, "For you remember, brothers, our labor and toil: we worked night and day, that we might not be a burden to any of you, while we proclaimed to you the gospel of God" (1 Thess 2:9). Of course, Paul was not trying to elevate working with one's hands above working with one's mind or vice versa. Rather, he was teaching that those who are able to labor, no matter the type of work, should labor to provide for themselves and for their families and not unnecessarily burden others. This was Paul's example for the people of God as he preached the gospel.

The Bible is full of illustrations, examples, and positive teachings about work. Consider that Jesus' parables often appeal to and include general examples of work: sowing, reaping, buying, selling, fishing, shepherding, investing, etc. Some familiar biblical passages with teachings about work include: "Whatever you do, work heartily, as for the Lord and not for men" (Col 3:23); "For even when we were with you, we would give you this command: If anyone is not willing to work, let him not eat" (2 Thess 3:10); and "The laborer deserves his wages" (1 Tim 5:18). Clearly, then, both in example and in teaching, the Bible addresses the topic of work, oftentimes in a commending manner and always with a positive outlook.

Misconceptions about Work

In spite of the descriptions and depictions of work in the Bible, many of us continue to hold misconceptions about it. As mentioned at the beginning of this chapter, it seems that many people—including Christians—default to the notion that work is bad and leisure is good. Some people view work as a necessary evil to earn income. We see this in how people talk about their employment, relish holidays and weekends, and dream of retirement. From this perspective, work becomes a means to an end: We work to live, and we live to play on the weekends to the degree we can afford it.

I am not trying to deny or ignore the real difficulties work sometimes brings or the benefits of rest (we'll talk more about rest in the next chapter). Indeed, our labors can sometimes be a daily grind. Regardless of our occupations, we all have seasons when work seems to be a boring, pointless, frustrating, exhausting, and thankless task. The Bible tells us that work has now become toil, the creation is cursed, and experience testifies that many of our coworkers are indifferent (or even hostile) to Christianity. Understandably, then, many people feel a lack of purpose in their work, second-guess their job choices, are unsure about their career trajectory, and often feel insecure in their employment. Sin in the workplace is real—both in ourselves and in our coworkers—and we can all attest to having experienced this in the fallen world.

Yet grappling with the inevitable effects of sin on our work is different than categorically viewing all work as bad and all leisure as good. The Bible describes work as a joyous privilege, not as a grudging necessity. God is a worker, and he made humanity to work. In fact, our daily labor is one of the most important ways in which we can functionally bear the image of God in the material world. Misunderstanding this concept will have grave practical consequences: Rather than being masters of our work, we will become its slaves; rather than ruling over our work, our work will rule over us. This is not God's plan or design for his children.

Another misconception about work in contemporary culture relates to the types of labor in which we are employed. For example, many people view service-based jobs as being inherently inferior to knowledge-based jobs. This is a wrong perspective, for while Scripture does prohibit certain types of employment—such as prostitution, assassination, or thievery—the Bible places no favor upon specific types of labor that are morally permissible. Some jobs naturally require more manual labor, while others require more mental labor. Scripture is not prejudiced, one way or the other, in regard to service-based jobs or knowledge-based jobs.

A related distortion about work is our tendency to favor higher-paying jobs (and sometimes those who hold them) over lower-paying jobs. For instance, when someone speaks of a desire to find "a good job," more often than not they mean a highly paying job. Low-paying jobs generally are not coveted. But practically speaking, it seems the definition of a good job should be one that meets an individual's natural abilities, educational preparation, life experience, and spiritual giftedness—regardless of the salary. This is not to say that income is an unimportant consideration. Indeed, compensation for production is not only important, but may also be a matter of justice (we'll revisit this in chapter 4). Yet to view higher-paying jobs as essentially superior to lower-paying jobs is a misconception.

Scripture's objectivity toward types of work also applies to the distinction often drawn between sacred and secular employment. It's easy to see how those who have "sacred" jobs, such as pastors and missionaries, are doing the Lord's work. It's much more difficult to connect secular jobs with kingdom work. Yet it's important to understand that this division between so-called sacred and secular employment is not found in Scripture. Certainly the work of the clergy is functionally different than the work of the laity, but the same could be said in comparing any two types or categories of work. The Bible teaches that regardless of the type(s) of work in which we are employed, all believers are a part of a royal priesthood (1 Pet 2:9), are engaged in kingdom work (Luke 11:2), and are to labor for the glory of God (1 Cor 10:31). Thus, both pastor and plumber are doing the Lord's work.

Although recognizing some of the more prevalent misconceptions about work is important, it would be impossible for us to delineate and analyze all such personal and cultural errors. But a sure way to identify and correct any distortion of Christian doctrine is to focus on what the Bible actually teaches. With this in mind, we'll turn to understanding the scriptural bases for labor to give us a perspective from which to address any mischaracterization of the doctrine of work.

Foundations of Work

In Genesis 1 we learn that God made human beings with material as well as spiritual components. He made man out "of dust from the ground and breathed into his nostrils the breath [or spirit] of life" (Gen 2:7). The teaching that human beings consist of body and spirit is repeated and developed all throughout Scripture in many different contexts (Matt 10:28; 2 Cor 7:1; Col 2:5; Jas 2:26). So, in the beginning, God made man a composite unity, a material/spiritual being, and placed him in the created realm within the garden of Eden.

That humanity has a spirit is one of the ways in which we are like God, for "God is spirit" (John 4:24). Yet in possessing a physical or material body, we are fundamentally unlike God the Father. This is one of the innumerable ways in which we have been made "a little lower than the heavenly beings" (Psa 8:5). Later, though, at the incarnation, Jesus took on a material body, thus becoming like us (Heb 2:14). The Gospels tell us Christ has a resurrected physical body (Luke 24:39), the same type of glorified material body believers will one day receive (Rom 8:11; Phil 3:21; 1 John 3:2). Having a physical body, then, cannot be inherently bad. In fact, as God declared at the conclusion of his creation, the material realm, including man's physical body, is very good.

Since we have material bodies, we naturally have material needs. The good news is that God has made provision within his creation to meet humanity's material needs. For example, before the fall, God situated Adam and Eve in a presumably temperate environment and gave them the fruit of the trees for food (Gen 1:29; 2:9). Later, after the fall,

God gave them animal skins for clothing and meat for food (Gen 3:21; 9:3). On further reflection, it seems amazing—indeed, it must be a mark of God's foreknowledge and grace—that he would build into the pre-fall world the resources necessary to meet humanity's postfall material needs, such as clothing and shelter.

One of the significant points of the creation narrative is that, of all the living beings God made, only people were given a job and directed to work. The animals were given permission to breed and to roam the earth, but only Adam was given an explicit, divine command to "be fruitful and multiply" (Gen 1:28). Beyond this, Adam was assigned the tasks of tilling the ground, tending the garden of Eden, and naming the animals (Gen 2:15, 19). Remember, this labor was all prescribed before the fall; thus, it was part of the divine blueprint for humanity and was inherently good.

Christianity is different from all other world religions in that it does not teach that sin entered the world after a golden age of leisure, nor does it teach that the afterlife will include the cessation of labor. Indeed, in the ancient biblical world, Christianity must have seemed odd in its view of work. The Roman gods were divine rulers, the Greek gods were philosopher-kings, and the Judeo-Christian God was a carpenter. We must understand the nature of God and man, as well as the foundational design for work, because true freedom is the ability to do what we were created to do—to function in accord with our nature, working to meet our own material needs.

Turning back to the creation narrative, another highly significant teaching is that "God created man in his own image, in the image of God he created him" (Gen 1:27). The concept of the image of God is a complex theological issue that stretches well beyond the scope of this book and the focus of this chapter. With this in mind, we'll focus on one part of this important biblical teaching—the functional aspect of image-bearing. In short, since God made us in his own image, God expects us to act like him. How can we accomplish this monumental task?

After creating us in his own image, the Bible relates that God gave humanity two specific tasks at which to labor. The first was to procreate—that is, to multiply and bear children (Gen 1:28). If we reflect on this command apart from our familiarity with the text, the instruction to multiply may seem odd. Think about this for a moment. Of all the possible commands God could have given, why did he charge Adam and Eve with procreation? Wouldn't they have done so anyway? God could have given humanity any directive, yet he chose to command procreation. Why? The opening chapters of Genesis are about God's work of creation; therefore, after making Adam and Eve in his own image, God essentially told them, "Bear my image. Function like me. Create." God is creator, and his image-bearers are commanded to pro-create.

The second task God gave Adam and Eve was to subdue the earth and to "have dominion over the fish of the sea and over the birds of the heavens and over every living thing that moves on the earth" (Gen 1:28). As with the command to procreate, so the task to exercise dominion has its roots in us being created in the image of God. Since the Lord is sovereign over all things, and since he created humanity in his own image, he then directed his image-bearers to function like him in exercising dominion (or sovereignty) over the creation.

By engaging in these two areas of labor—procreation and dominion—we can functionally bear the image of God. This is what we were designed to do. This is what brings satisfaction to people and glory to God. But we must not limit the scope of these two tasks to the obvious applications of childbearing and exercising authority. Fundamentally speaking, procreation is the creation and fostering of human relationships; this is manifested in childbearing within marriage. However, viewed more widely, procreation entails creating and fostering relationships in various social contexts, including families, churches, schools, cities, governments, and so on. In this sense, the duty to procreate can be applied culture-wide. This is part of our work.

In a basic sense, exercising dominion entails creating order out of chaos or bringing direction to that which is aimless. As with procreation, so the scope of exercising dominion is vast and culture-wide. In regard to human relationships, exercising dominion may involve cultivating leadership, providing order, or exercising self-control. Concerning the natural world, exercising dominion may include building infrastructure, developing agriculture, domesticating animals, enhancing education, furthering the arts, and countless other contexts in which order and direction are needed.

These directives to exercise dominion and to procreate are often referred to as the "cultural mandate."

When we apply the cultural mandate spiritually within the fallen world, the resulting paradigm is what theologians call the Great Commission (Matt 28:19–20). The work of evangelism is, in a sense, procreation of spiritual life as people are born again. Similarly, exercising dominion over sin and bringing order to all areas of a believer's life is the process of spiritual maturity or personal discipleship. But before we discuss the fallen world in which we labor at evangelism and discipleship, we need to review the distortion of work.

Distortion of Work

As we've discussed, work is not the result of humanity's sinfulness but is part of God's good, divine design for his creation. The fall affected the spiritual and the material aspects of human existence. In a basic sense, sin is a denial that we are made in the image of God. Ironically, such a denial can lead us to attempt to remake God in our own image. When we sin, we proclaim ourselves to be gods; we deny our divine dependence; and we try to abdicate all that image-bearing entails—often including our duty to work. This situation is further complicated in that, on account of our sin, the physical environment is now cursed. Sin and its curse not only make us less inclined to work, they make work more difficult. One result of the fall, then, is a radical distortion of work.

In the cursed world of fallen people, work often becomes toil. We may grapple with a tendency to be lazy. Knowing this inclination, the author of Proverbs 6:10–11 warns, "A little sleep, a little slumber, a little folding of the hands to rest, and poverty will come upon you like a robber, and want like an armed man." At other times we struggle with overworking, which we can see as a temptation to place our security in our own labor and accumulated resources rather than in God. Again, Proverbs admonishes us: "Do not toil to acquire wealth; be discerning enough to desist" (Prov 23:4). Other common distortions of work include the temptation to misrepresent our own work and to take credit for the work of others.

Corporate-level work is also distorted in the fallen world. The workplace has ethical dilemmas, personal tensions, employee exploitation, defrauding of customers, stealing from employers, and shady advertising, among many other society-wide labor issues. Moreover, entire areas of commerce have arisen that are inherently evil—designed to incite sin, to prey upon the weak, and to destroy traditional societal institutions. Examples include the pornography, abortion, gambling, and sex trafficking industries, just to name a few. Clearly, God's good design for work has been distorted by sin.

This distortion should not surprise us, though; God foretold this outcome of our sin. After the fall, our first divine duty became more difficult. As God told Eve, "I will surely multiply your pain in childbearing; in pain you shall bring forth children. Your desire shall be for your husband, and he shall rule over you" (Gen 3:16). Married couples experience the effect of the fall on procreation as they struggle with difficulty conceiving, pain in childbirth, and disorder in gender roles. The same types of challenges are manifest beyond marriage, as meaningful human relationships are difficult to create and to maintain. This is true even in Christian families and in churches.

God also spoke of the difficulties we would have in our second divinely assigned task—exercising dominion over the world. After the fall God said, "Cursed is the ground because of you; in pain you shall eat of it all the days of your life; thorns and thistles it shall bring forth for you; and you shall eat the plants of the field. By the sweat of your face you shall eat bread, till you return to the ground, for out of it you were taken; for you are dust, and to dust you shall return" (Gen 3:17–19). We now meet resistance as we try to instill order and develop the potential of the material world. At times, this makes work hard, unproductive, frustrating, and inefficient. Such is the impact of sin on our labor.

So, while God made us to work, our work is now distorted. We face the triple challenge of our own sinful hearts, the sinfulness of others with whom we work, and the curse on the created order itself. The distortion of work is one of the reasons "the whole creation has been groaning together in the pains of childbirth until now. And not only the creation, but we ourselves, who have the firstfruits of the Spirit, groan inwardly as we wait eagerly for adoption as sons, the redemption of our bodies" (Rom 8:22–23). We long for restoration.

Restoration of Work

But we have hope. In the context of the passage that references the groaning of both humanity and creation as caused by sin, Paul refers to the "hope that the creation itself will be set free from its bondage to corruption and obtain the freedom of the glory of the children of God" (Rom 8:20–21). Further reading in both the Old and New Testaments reveals that the Bible speaks of a new heavens and a new earth, where sin will be eradicated and we will be able to work unimpeded by sin, free to manifest the image of God (Psa 102:25–26; Isa 65:17–25; 66:22–23; 2 Pet 3:12–13; Rev 21:1–22:5).

The scriptural teaching of a new heavens and new earth is a beautiful doctrine—one that helps us understand the scope of God's plan of redemption, which includes the salvation of humanity and the purging of the entire created order of the effects of sin. Indeed, redemption is no less comprehensive than the fall. Creation and redemption are not at odds. Jesus did not become incarnate to remove humanity from the material world, but rather to deliver us from sin so that we can glorify God and labor in accord with his creational design—all in the context of a restored heavens and earth.

Although the Bible often references this restoration, details about the new heavens and new earth are sparse. They will be new in the sense of "fresh" or "redeemed," not new in the sense of "original" or "created." In 2 Peter 3:13 and Revelation 21:2, the term rendered as "new" is a word that refers to nature or quality, not to essence or being. Think about it like this: Just as Christians have new life yet remain the same beings (albeit waiting for glorified, material bodies), so the new heavens and new earth will be the current heavens and earth made new. In his discussion of the new heavens and new earth, Peter cites Noah's flood as an example of this pattern of renewal (2 Pet 3:1-13).

The Bible also doesn't give much information about the specifics of humanity's future work. We do know that in the future cosmos, we will no longer procreate within the context of marriage, for Jesus taught the Sadducees, "When [human beings] rise from the dead, they neither marry nor are given in marriage" (Mark 12:25). However, in the new heavens and new earth, people will still procreate nonsexually in the sense of forming and fostering new relationships. Indeed, the new cosmos will include a nearly innumerable company of believers from throughout history.

In regard to exercising dominion over the new heavens and new earth, Scripture gives more details about the creation itself than it does about our work within the creation. The Bible reports that deserts will bloom and there will be trees, vineyards, and precious stones (Isa 35:1-7; 65:21; Ezek 47:7, 12; Rev 2:7; 21:18-21; 22:2, 14, 19). Scripture teaches that the restored earth will also include animals such as the wolf, lamb, leopard, goat, cow, calf, lion, bear, ox, cobra, viper, and serpent (Isa 11:6-8; 65:22-25). Presumably, among our other endeavors, our work in the new cosmos will entail tending to the plants and interacting with the animals, as it was in the garden of Eden (Isa 2:4).

The Value of Work

Work is foundational to human existence—the divine design of work goes back to creation, and its practice extends forward throughout eternity. Although work has been distorted by the fall, it will one day be possible to labor according to our creational design, at the time of "restoring all the things" (Acts 3:21). Work will be manifest perfectly in our future, yet it holds value in the here and now. Its value is both intrinsic (or inherent) and instrumental.

The intrinsic value of work is the goodness or value of work itself. Since we are image-bearers of God, it is good for us to work—work resonates with our creational design and models God, who is a worker. This is one reason work can be so fulfilling. Just as God takes delight in his work (Gen 1:31), so we will ultimately find delight in our labors. In teaching on the intrinsic value of work, the author of Ecclesiastes says:

> There is nothing better for a person than that he should eat and drink and find enjoyment in his toil. This also, I saw, is from the hand of God, for apart from him who can eat or who can have enjoyment? ... So I saw that there is nothing better than that a man should rejoice in his work, for that is his lot (Eccl 2:24–25; 3:22).

This is true for all people, and especially for those who realize the divine design of labor and who are in relationship with its designer.

Work also has instrumental value, as seen in what work accomplishes or produces. More often than not, this is the way we perceive and measure the value of work. The products of our labor allow God to provide for the material needs of his creation, including us (Titus 3:14), our families (1 Tim 5:8), and others (Eph 4:28). In addition, work often draws us into relationships as we develop the collaborative potential of creation. Both products and relationships demonstrate the instrumental value of labor.

Scripture often appeals to the instrumental value of work as incentive. Proverbs teaches, "He who gathers by labor will increase" (Prov 13:11 NKJV), and Paul says, "If anyone is not willing to work, let him not eat" (2 Thess 3:10). In biblical times, the instrumental value of work was so important that events such as planting a vineyard without yet enjoying its produce was cause to be excused from military service (Deut 20:6). Conversely, the Old Testament frequently refers to work without production, or without the enjoyment of production, as a threat or curse (Lev 26:16; Deut 28:30, 33, 38–42; Job 31:8; Psa 109:11; Prov 5:9–11; Jer 5:17; Mic 6:15).

The Doctrine of Vocation

With our understanding of the foundations, distortion, restoration, and value of work, we might logically ask, "How or at what shall I work?" Answering this question leads us to examine the doctrine of vocation.

The term "vocation" comes from the Latin word *vocare*, which means "to call." The doctrine of vocation is the concept that everyone is called to a certain type of work.

Note that vocations are not necessarily specific jobs, but rather are what could be called stations in life. Moreover, vocations are not always tied to a paycheck, and most people hold multiple vocations simultaneously. Examples of vocations include a government office holder, an employer in business, a manufacturing employee, a neighbor, a spouse, a roommate, or a religious leader, among many others.

Each vocation has its own sphere of work, authority, responsibility, and duties. What is permissible in one vocation may be prohibited in another. For example, sexual intercourse is permissible for spouses within the sphere of marriage, but is prohibited between unmarried coworkers in the sphere of business. Likewise, capital punishment is permissible for certain employees of the state, while killing human beings is immoral for those in most other vocations. Moreover, the duties and authority attendant to each vocation are tied to a specific sphere and are not contingent on the worthiness of the person who fills it.

God uses vocations to care for and rule the world. We often err in thinking of God as being far above the created order or residing solely within us. Given the repetitive patterns of life, it can be tempting to believe that the world runs on its own, and we often neglect to think of God as presently and continually working in the world through his people in ordinary ways. This concept that God works through vocations is tied to the doctrine of providence. The term "providence" comes from a Latin word meaning "to provide." Martin Luther rightly said that vocations are the mask of God through which he provides for the world.

This idea that God providentially serves the world, meeting material needs through our vocational work, may seem odd to some people. Believers are more accustomed to thinking of their own service to the Lord in their vocations. While it's true that we are to serve God, it's also true that part of God's unfolding plan is to serve us. Jesus said, "The Son of Man came not to be served but to serve, and to give his life as a ransom for many" (Matt 20:28); "I am among you as the one who serves" (Luke 22:27). Thankfully, God's provision for us through vocations is not contingent on our assent. God can use the business owner who is motivated solely by profit to employ people and to provide goods for the community. In so doing, God providentially cares for humanity.

We can also think about vocations as a means by which we can love and serve our neighbor. The various vocations in a given community create a vast interchange of work and a division of labor through which people are continually giving to and receiving from one another. This exchange of vocations—what we call the economy—is a basic element of the fabric of society. Of course, not all vocations entail love and service to others. Drug dealers, contract killers, and con men work to harm their neighbors rather than help them. It's also possible to sin within a serving vocation—for instance, politicians who exploit rather than serve or doctors who kill rather than heal. But carried out as God intended, vocations entail love of and service to neighbors.

This brings us back to our question, "How or at what shall I work?" Our answer should consider that each individual likely has several different vocations to fulfill, simultaneously, in different spheres of life. As to the specific types of work we ought to pursue, we can look to factors such as spiritual gifts, talents, experience, preparation, and opportunity for direction. The right labor to pursue at any given time is the work that considers as many of these factors as possible, loves and serves our neighbors, and is a means for God to provide for the good world that he made.

Heading Forward

God made us to work in the material world, and this divine design persists despite the presence of sin. Through our work, God provides for our material needs as well as for the needs of our neighbors. And while this is good, Scripture also teaches that God did not design us to work all day, every day. Just as God designed us to work, so he also designed us to rest; we will turn to the topic of Sabbath in the next chapter.

Summary

- Those who are able to work should labor to provide for themselves and for their families. This is God's good design for humanity.

- The Bible does not favor service-based jobs or knowledge-based jobs, nor does it distinguish between so-called secular employment and sacred employment.

- Working and procreating are two ways in which humanity bears the image of God in the material world.

Carrying out these duties is often referred to as the cultural mandate.

- Work has both an intrinsic value (seen in our design) and an instrumental value (seen in our production).

- Everyone is called to labor at a vocation. Through vocations God provides for the world, and people can love and serve their neighbors.

Action Points

- Have you ever had a job that you would consider a dream job? What made it a dream job?

- What makes work meaningful? How do you measure success in your work?

- How is work connected to the spiritual realm?

CHAPTER 3

Rest and Sabbath

Rest and Sabbath. What do you think about these concepts? For many Christians, the idea of Sabbath brings to mind legalistic thoughts and uneasy questions about what a person can and cannot do on the Sabbath—whether it's okay to go out for lunch on the Sabbath and be served by a restaurant employee, whether housework or yard work are permissible on the Sabbath, and so on. And what day is the Sabbath anyway: Saturday or Sunday? Many Christians agree that the Bible discusses the Sabbath, but they are unsure about (and perhaps even afraid of learning) what it means. It's almost as if some people want to affirm the commandments—or at least nine of them—so long as they can omit the moral law concerning the Sabbath. But rest is a large component of living in the material world.

We have already discussed our seemingly inherent love of rest. Sometimes we love rest too much, and we idolize weekends, vacations, and future retirement. Consequently, we are prone to misunderstand or even demonize the concept of work. But when we view work properly, we will see it as God's design for us and, thus, as something to be embraced. In a similar manner, in this chapter we'll see that rest and the Sabbath are not to be idolized or feared but that they, too, are part of our creational design. Just like labor, rest is a way in which mankind can functionally bear the image of God. In fact, when God first gave the Ten Commandments in the book of Exodus, he appealed to his own rest as the pattern and rationale for his people's rest (see Exod 20:8–11).

Since we live in the material world, everything we do involves either work or rest. It's important, then, that we grasp the concepts of rest and Sabbath. We'll begin by looking at these through the lens of the fourth of the Ten Commandments, which is the moral law concerning Sabbath-keeping. We'll then turn our attention to a review of some of the wealth- and poverty-related laws God gave his people in the Old Testament. As we'll see, rest and Sabbath are the foundation of many of God's economic laws.

The Fourth Commandment

The fourth commandment, which first appears in Exodus 20:8–11 and is reiterated in Deuteronomy 5:12–15, is the longest of the commandments. To summarize: "Remember the Sabbath day, to keep it holy" (Exod 20:8). This law is the first commandment in the Ten Commandments stated positively and is one of only two commandments—the other being the fifth—with a positive formulation. By positive formulation, I mean the fourth commandment does not contain "thou shalt not." With this moral law, God is not trying to legalistically prevent us from happiness; rather, he is lovingly empowering us to manifest his image.

Another significant aspect of the fourth commandment is that it is the only one of the Ten Commandments that differs in the Exodus and Deuteronomy narratives—not in content, but in the motivation God provides for keeping the commandment. In Exodus the fourth commandment is rooted in God's rest at creation, while in Deuteronomy it is connected to God's redemption of Israel from slavery in Egypt. This association between rest and redemption is important for understanding and applying this commandment.

Believers are often unsure how to apply the Sabbath commandment to their everyday lives. Disagreements about the fourth commandment are usually related to defining the concept of Sabbath itself. While some Christians affirm Sabbath-keeping, others hold that the notion is equivalent to legalism and believe that the practice quenches Christian liberty. Yet if the Sabbath is part of the eternal moral law, then keeping it (or violating it) is just as important as keeping (or violating) any of the other Ten Commandments. It is important, then, that we arrive at a proper understanding of the Sabbath—first by defining it and then by discerning the temporary or eternal nature of the concept.

Defining the Sabbath

Interestingly, the primary meaning of the term "Sabbath" is not "seven," as many people assume, but "rest." The word Sabbath comes from a Hebrew verb that means "to rest or to cease from labor." The fourth commandment specifies that people were to observe this Sabbath rest every seventh day. Because God rested on the seventh day of creation, the Hebrew word for Sabbath came to be used for the number seven as well as for the seventh day of the week. However, the number and day were named after the act of resting, not vice versa. So in Scripture the ideas of rest and Sabbath are nearly identical.

In Old Testament times, the concept of Sabbath-keeping, or regularly resting in order to worship, was deeply entrenched in the life of God's people. The Jewish culture and civil system manifested the Sabbath with a weekly observance of the Sabbath day. This day of rest is prescribed in the fourth commandment, but it is also referred to in passages such as Exodus 23:12 and Leviticus 23:3. The idea of Sabbath-keeping was also demonstrated in the Sabbatical Year, which was to be celebrated every seventh year (Exod 23:10–11; Lev 25:1–7; Deut 15:1–11). Moreover, the Sabbath concept can be seen in the Year of Jubilee (Lev 25:8–55; 27:16–25), which was a special celebration designed to be observed every 50th year, or after seven cycles of the Sabbatical Year. We'll revisit these civil manifestations of the Sabbath toward the end of this chapter.

Yet the question remains as to whether the Sabbath is an eternally valid part of God's moral law. Does Scripture support the temporary or eternal nature of the Sabbath? A survey of the Bible reveals several pieces of evidence in support of the idea that Sabbath-keeping is a component of the eternal moral law of God.

The Eternal Sabbath

Scripture first mentions resting on the seventh day in the creation narrative of Genesis 2:1–3:

> Thus the heavens and the earth were finished, and all the host of them. And on the seventh day God finished his work that he had done, and he rested on the seventh day from all his work that he had done. So God blessed the seventh day and made it holy, because on it God rested from all his work that he had done in creation.

Interestingly, God rested even though the Bible teaches that he does not tire or sleep (Psa 121:4; Isa 40:28). Let's examine this passage more carefully.

In Exodus 20:8–11, the fourth commandment appeals to God's rest at creation and his sanctifying of the seventh day in Genesis 2:1–3 as a basis for people to keep the Sabbath. This grounding of the fourth commandment in creation is important, for here God appeals to his own example, prior to the fall, as a pattern. Drawing upon our discussion of being image-bearers of God, we could express the rationale for Sabbath-keeping like this: Since God made man in his own image and then rested, we, being image-bearers of God, should rest. In keeping the Sabbath, then, humanity can functionally bear the image of God. Since Sabbath-keeping is a pattern set by God and is a means by which we can bear the image of God, we would assume the practice to be eternally valid, practically necessary, and personally fulfilling.

Interestingly, the Sabbath is the only impersonal object or event that God blesses in Scripture. Nothing in Genesis 2:1–3 indicates this blessing was temporary or applicable only to the then-nonexistent nation of Israel. On the contrary, the grounding of the fourth commandment in the events of creation leads to the conclusion that God's rest at the end of creation week was an example for all of humanity. The Lord's Sabbath observance was a firstfruits of sorts: In resting and blessing the seventh day, He was demonstrating a chronological pattern by which the world could be regulated.

The eternal nature of the Sabbath is also supported by humanity's observance of a seven-day week since creation. Scripture refers to such units of seven days repeatedly (e.g., Gen 7:4, 10; 8:10, 12; 29:27; 31:23; 50:10). Since we, too, observe a seven-day week, we may not find this all that unusual—but it's part of the pattern set by God, a pattern that included the Sabbath, a day that God had blessed and made holy (Gen 2:3).

We find further support for the Sabbath being part of the eternal moral law in the reference to Cain and Abel offering sacrifices "in the course of time" (Gen 4:3). According to *Young's Literal Translation*, this Hebrew phrase can be rendered "at the end of days," which raises the question, "At the end of *what* days?" A logical conclusion is that Cain and Abel were worshiping God by offering sacrifices at the end of the days of the week—that is, on the day that later became known as the Sabbath. So, then, it seems that humanity has always observed a regular, weekly time of rest and worship (see Job 1:5; 2:13).

Perhaps the best evidence for Sabbath-keeping as an eternally valid concept appears in Exodus 16:23-30, in God's instructions to Moses for collecting manna in the wilderness—which took place prior to the giving of the Ten Commandments at Sinai. In this passage God tells Moses, "The LORD has given you the Sabbath; therefore on the sixth day he gives you bread for two days. Remain each of you in his place; let no one go out of his place on the seventh day" (Exod 16:29). Note that God does not provide a detailed explanation of the Sabbath; Moses would have already been familiar with the concept. This familiarity with the Sabbath also helps explain why God says in the fourth commandment to "remember the Sabbath" (Exod 20:8), implying they already had knowledge of the practice.

In the New Testament the eternal, moral nature of the Sabbath can be seen in the life and teaching of Jesus. The Gospels report that Jesus faithfully kept the Sabbath, even declaring himself to be "lord of the Sabbath" (Matt 12:8; Luke 6:5). Although no charge of Sabbath-breaking was brought up at Jesus' trial, during his ministry he was repeatedly confronted by religious leaders who accused him of breaking the Sabbath. Each time, Jesus responded to the charge by showing that the error lay with the leaders' misunderstanding of the Sabbath, not with his or his disciples' actions (see Matt 12:1-13; Mark 2:23-3:5; Luke 6:1-10). I believe many people in the modern church also misunderstand the Sabbath—their misconception often-times leading to their opposition.

Jesus made one of his most important statements on the Sabbath during one of these confrontations with the religious leaders, as recorded at Mark 2:23-28. On this occasion, Jesus declared, "The Sabbath was made for man, not man for the Sabbath" (Mark 2:27). So rather than teaching against the Sabbath when he was accused of breaking it, Jesus affirmed the Sabbath as a good thing: an event made by God for humanity. The author of the book of Hebrews affirms Jesus' teaching on the relevance of the Sabbath, saying, "So then, there remains a Sabbath rest for the people of God" (Heb 4:9). Of course, we would expect such teachings if Sabbath-keeping is in accord with humanity's creational design and is a means by which we can functionally bear the image of God.

We should note that the Old Testament prophets refer to the Sabbath in the context of the new heavens and the new earth. For example, Isaiah prophesies,

> For as the new heavens and the new earth
>   that I make
> shall remain before me, says the LORD,
>   so shall your offspring and your name remain.
> From new moon to new moon,
>   and from Sabbath to Sabbath,
> all flesh shall come to worship before me,
> declares the LORD (Isa 66:22-23; see also Ezek 46:1-12; Matt 24:20).

If the Sabbath is part of God's creational design, is included in the moral law, and will be observed for eternity on the new earth, it seems likely that God intended the Sabbath to remain in effect in our modern context.

In arguing that the Sabbath is not part of God's eternal moral law and is not binding on Christians, some people have appealed to passages including Romans 14:5, Galatians 4:9-11, and Colossians 2:16-17. Yet the context of these passages reveals that they most likely refer to the Jewish civil and ceremonial laws, not to the moral law of God. In each passage, Paul confronts a group of false teachers known as the Judaizers. These false teachers argued for a works-based salvation in an effort to impose Jewish civil and ceremonial laws on the church. Paul teaches that Jewish civil and ceremonial laws do not apply to Christians, especially as a means of sanctification. His teaching was affirmed by the first church council, as reported in Acts 15:1-29.

Properly defined, the Sabbath is fundamentally about rest, and it is an eternally relevant concept. However, we must keep in mind that rest is not synonymous with inactivity. Indeed, someone may be inactive because they are unable to work (such as being disabled), or they may be inactive because they are in sin (such as being lazy). This is not the kind of rest prescribed in the fourth commandment. The Sabbath commandment relates rest to holiness and worship. In the moral law, God instructed his people to "keep [the Sabbath] holy" (Exod 20:8; Deut 5:12). Let's explore the practical dimensions of this command in more depth.

Keeping the Sabbath

We've learned that the fourth commandment is an eternal moral law of God that calls us to a type of holy rest and worship. We have yet to explore how the Sabbath applies to and is manifest in daily living. Recall that the fourth commandment appeals to God's rest in the Exodus narrative (Exod 20:11) and to his redemption of Israel from Egyptian slavery in the Deuteronomy narrative (Deut 5:15). In appealing to these factors God reminded his people of both his promise and their identity. God's promise is eternal life (or rest) in Christ, and the identity of his followers is that of people who have been chosen and redeemed from the bondage of sin.

As applied to the Israelites, the Sabbath pictured the eternal rest and redemption that was promised at the Messiah's coming. God's people were to keep the Sabbath, then, as a reminder to themselves and as a demonstration to the world of who they were and whose they were. The Sabbath was a practical manifestation of their future hope (eternal rest) and of how to attain it (by resting—that is, having faith—in God). Indeed, God instructed Moses to teach the Israelites that the Sabbath "is a sign between me and you throughout your generations, that you may know that I, the LORD, sanctify you" (Exod 31:13; see Isa 56:4-7). Furthermore, through the Prophet Ezekiel, God declared, "I gave them my Sabbaths, as a sign between me and them, that they might know that I am the LORD who sanctifies them" (Ezek 20:12).

In a similar manner, for Christians the Sabbath is a sign of redemption and, as such, it depicts the eternal rest we have received from Jesus in salvation. Just as it was a reminder to Israel in the Old Testament, Sabbath is a reminder to the New Testament Church both of our identity as blood-bought sinners and of God's promise of eternal rest in him. As sinners, we are prone to forget these important gospel truths. Therefore, in his grace, God gave us the Sabbath so that we will not forget the implications and extent of the gospel.

All facets of the moral law have both broad and specific applications. In a broad sense, Christians are to keep the Sabbath all day, every day, as we live lives characterized by hope, trust, and resting in the Lord—not by worry and anxiety. This is what Jesus taught when he said,

> Therefore do not be anxious, saying, "What shall we eat?" or "What shall we drink?" or "What shall we wear?" For the Gentiles seek after all these things, and your heavenly Father knows that you need them all. But seek first the kingdom of God and his righteousness, and all these things will be added to you. Therefore do not be anxious about tomorrow, for tomorrow will be anxious for itself. Sufficient for the day is its own trouble (Matt 6:31–34; see also Matt 11:28–30).

In a specific sense the fourth commandment calls believers to observe a regular day of worship—a day Christians have historically called the "Lord's Day" (see Psa 118:24). This ought to be a day on which God's people can gather together to rest in God, worship him, and corporately express thanksgiving for the redemption he supplies (see Heb

10:25). Keeping the Sabbath in this specific sense should not be a legalistic burden, characterized by lists of allowed and forbidden activities. Rather, the Sabbath should be a joyous celebration and a blessing, for it gives us a chance to rest from our toils, to assemble together, and to functionally bear the image of God. This is why God instructs his people to "call the Sabbath a delight and the holy day of the LORD honorable" (Isa 58:13).

Jesus offers the ideal example of biblical Sabbath-keeping (in a specific sense). The Gospels record that on the Sabbath Jesus attended the synagogue, taught the Bible, healed the sick, and fellowshiped with his disciples (Matt 12:1–13; Mark 1:21–34; 2:23–28; 6:1–11; Luke 4:16–30; 6:6–10; 13:10–17). As believers today, we are still to follow Christ's example, keeping the Sabbath by engaging in works of worship, works of service, works of mercy, and works of fellowship.

As with other aspects of the moral law, there are practical benefits to keeping the Sabbath. Resting from work prevents us from making work our ultimate source of security and affords us the opportunity to rely on and to worship God. Moreover, resting from work allows us to enjoy what we have produced by our labor (see Eccl 2:17–26) and helps mitigate the effects of the fall, which turned work into toil (see Gen 3:19). These benefits, and the gospel-centric nature of Sabbath, should prevent us from seeing Sabbath-keeping as a laborious duty. Rather, it should be a natural desire of our hearts both to reflect on and to enjoy the eternal rest and redemption made possible through the cross.

Saturday or Sunday?

If we seek to keep the Sabbath in a specific sense, we must question the correct day of observance. Indeed, to answer this important question, we need to know both what the Sabbath entails and when (in a specific sense) to keep it. The Old Testament is clear that the Israelites kept the Sabbath on the seventh day of the week, Saturday. In the New Testament, the early church moved the day of Sabbath observance to the first day of the week, Sunday. For example, Luke reports that the church at Troas gathered together to break bread and to hear Paul preach "on the first day of the week" (Acts 20:7). Similarly, Paul instructs the church in Corinth, "On the first day of every week, each of you is to put something aside and store it up, as he may prosper, so that there will be no collecting when I come" (1 Cor 16:2). John refers to Sunday as "the Lord's Day" (Rev 1:10; see Psa 118:24). The day on which the early church rested and worshiped was Sunday—but why did the day of Sabbath observance change?

Perhaps one factor in the early church's decision to move the day of Sabbath observance from Saturday to Sunday was the Jewish heritage of many early converts. Since the Jewish Sabbath was both a religious observance and a cultural event, it is likely that many early Christians of Jewish descent would have wanted to continue observing the Sabbath in a Jewish cultural sense. Having the day of Christian rest, assembly, and worship on Sunday would have helped to accommodate such a desire and would have avoided creating unnecessary tension between Christian worship practices and the Jewish culture.

Although cultural and logistical factors contributed to the early church moving Sabbath observance to Sunday, in all likelihood, the main reason for the change was that all of Jesus' named postresurrection appearances occurred on Sunday (see Matt 28:9-10; Mark 16:12-14; Luke 24:13-51; John 20:11-23, 26-29; Rev 1:9-20). For the early church, it must have seemed quite logical to worship Jesus on the day of his continued appearances. Moreover, the promised Holy Spirit also came on a Sunday, the day of Pentecost (see Lev 23:15-16; Acts 2:1-4). In light of these factors, and with their realization that the Sabbath was not a day but a lifestyle and an event, the early church likely had no problem with moving the day of Sabbath observance.

The Civil Sabbath

In seeking to better understand and observe the Sabbath, it may be helpful to study the context in which God directed the Israelites to keep it. The Old Testament contains hundreds of regulations designed to provide order for all areas of Jewish society. While the civil laws of any nation are directly applicable only in the context in which they are given, legitimate civil regulations are ultimately time-bound cultural applications of unchanging moral laws. For example, in our own historical context, the civil law against vehicular speeding is valid because it is a contemporary, contextual application of the sixth commandment—that is, the moral law against murder or, stated conversely, the moral law exhorting us to respect human life.

Given its emphasis on rest from labor, the moral law concerning the Sabbath results in societal laws that are primarily economic in nature when applied in a civil context. In fact, the Old Testament contains dozens of regulations addressing the economic life of God's people, most of which relate (in one form or another) to the institution of the Sabbath. We recall that the Sabbath had three manifestations within the Hebrew culture and civil law: the Sabbath day (see Exod 20:8–11; 23:12; Lev 23:3; Deut 5:12–15), the Sabbatical Year (see Exod 23:10–11; Lev 25:1–7; Deut 15:1–18), and the Year of Jubilee (see Lev 25:8–55; 27:16–25).

The Sabbath Day

The Sabbath day was essentially a straightforward application of the fourth commandment. The civil law about the Sabbath day prescribed a cessation of ordinary labors, for both people and animals, one out of every seven days. The Sabbath day allowed the Israelites, their servants, and their animals to rest. Although this was not long-term rest, it nevertheless kept the Sabbath before the people and allowed for functional image-bearing. All of the major Jewish holidays and feasts were held on a Sabbath day, including Passover, the Feasts of Unleavened Bread, Firstfruits, Weeks, Trumpets, and Tabernacles, and the Day of Atonement (see Lev 23; Num 28–29).

The Sabbatical Year

The Sabbatical Year, which was to be observed every seventh year, was similar to the Sabbath day in that it allowed for rest among the Israelites, their servants, and their animals. However, the Sabbatical Year was unique in several ways. First, it allowed for the land to rest for an entire year. The civil law specified that during this year the land was to lie fallow, and the people and animals were to eat what grew of its own accord (see Exod 23:11; Lev 25:5-7). Obviously, the Sabbatical Year allowed for more extensive rest than did the weekly Sabbath day.

A second distinctive of the Sabbatical Year was that all financial debts between Jewish brethren—but not debts with foreigners—were to be released. The rationale for this is expressed in Deuteronomy 15:2: "because the LORD's release has been proclaimed" (see Deut 15:1-6). Scholars debate whether this release of debts entailed a complete cancellation of unpaid sums or a temporary suspension of payments. In either case, the release from debt functions as an extension of the prescribed motivation for keeping the Sabbath in Deuteronomy 5:15—that is, the release pictures freedom from the bondage of sin. While the civil law of the Sabbatical Year does not apply in our context, we, too, are to reflect the gospel in our economic dealings.

Scripture does not record the specific observance of the Sabbatical Year by the Jews, and this has sparked debate as to whether it was ever actually observed in Israel. As 2 Chronicles 36:21 indicates, the length of the

Babylonian captivity was determined by the Jews' neglect of the Sabbatical Year in accordance with God's warning in Leviticus 26:34-35. The Israelites were held in Babylon for 70 years (see Jer 25:12; 29:10), which would account for 490 years of neglected observance. It is no coincidence that a failure to rest in God (in a spiritual and practical sense) led Israel into bondage in Babylon (in a spiritual and practical sense).

The Year of Jubilee

The Year of Jubilee was to be observed every 50th year, after seven cycles of the Sabbatical Year. This was to be a yearlong Sabbath celebration in which the people, animals, and land ceased from labor and a proclamation of "liberty throughout the land to all its inhabitants" was declared (Lev 25:10). In fact, the term "jubilee" is derived from a Hebrew word meaning "joyful shout." Thus, the Year of Jubilee was a time to rest and rejoice in the freedom promised in the coming Messiah—freedom not from work but from sin, which is manifest in the fallen world through situations including financial bondage and slavery.

Unlike in the Sabbatical Year, during the Year of Jubilee, the people and animals were not to eat what grew freely from the land but instead from the excess provided by the Lord (Lev 25:11, 19). In the year before the Year of Jubilee, God promised to send a harvest large enough to last three years, thus allowing complete rest for people, animals, and land (Lev 25:20-22). The three years of produce would provide food for the seventh Sabbatical Year, the Year of Jubilee, and the following year (the first year in the new 50-year Jubilee cycle), during which the land that had lain fallow for two years would be reworked and replanted.

The specific laws regarding the Year of Jubilee may be divided up into three sections, the first of which pertains to redemption of land (Lev 25:8–28). The civil law specified that all land that had been sold since the last Year of Jubilee was to be returned to its original owner (Lev 25:13). This did not involve release of debt, as was the case in the Sabbatical Year, but expiration of loan terms. Land in Israel could not be sold permanently; it was effectively leased according to the number of years remaining until the next Jubilee (see Lev 25:14–16). The money exchanged in the "sale" of the land was not for the land itself, but for the land's potential produce. This reinforced the concept that people are stewards, not owners, of God's land.

A second category of laws related to the Year of Jubilee pertains to the redemption of houses. In Leviticus 25:29–34 we read that houses within unwalled villages were to be returned to their original owners at the Jubilee (Lev 25:31). Houses within walled towns or cities could be sold permanently (Lev 25:29–30). Since farmland reverted to its original owners, the houses on rural farmland reverted as well. This raises the question of why the sale of a house in a city was permanent. Given the Sabbath underpinning of the Jubilee, a possible explanation is that walled villages were an object lesson, picturing the rest and security available in Christ. Thus, once established, the stewardship of homes in towns and cities was permanent, like salvation.

REST AND SABBATH **63**

A final category of Jubilee laws relates to the redemption of slaves (Lev 25:35-55). In this passage the civil law states that Israelites who worked as indentured servants were to be set free in the Year of Jubilee (Lev 25:39-43, 47-55). Interestingly, however, foreigners did not have to be released (Lev 25:44-46). In all likelihood, God's people were freed under the Jubilee legislation as a picture of the eternal rest promised in salvation: The Jubilee foreshadowed redemption, and unbelievers will not be redeemed, so foreigners were not released during the Jubilee.

The various manifestations of the Sabbath within the Jewish civil law encompassed the resting of people, land, and animals, the reversion of land and houses to their original owners, and the freeing of Israelite slaves. In differing ways and to differing degrees, these events were all designed by God to communicate gospel truths related to rest and redemption.

Heading Forward

As we've learned, the Old Testament civil laws related to the Sabbath are primarily economic in nature. It's important to note that Sabbath-oriented civil laws did not entail redistribution of created wealth, income equality, or equalization of resources (i.e., animals, material wealth, grain or other harvest goods, tools, etc.). During the Year of Jubilee, houses and land were not redistributed to the poor but were returned to their original owners. These laws did not abolish private property but preserved the original distribution of private property and restored the opportunity to create wealth through resetting the means of production. With these foundational ideas in mind, we turn to a larger discussion of wealth and poverty.

Summary

- The primary meaning of the term "Sabbath" is not "seven" but "rest." The Sabbath day was named after the act of resting, not vice versa.

- God's appeal in Genesis 2:1–3 to his own rest as a basis for Sabbath-keeping emphasizes that observing the Sabbath is a way in which we can functionally bear God's image.

- The rest prescribed in the Sabbath should not be confused with inactivity. Sabbath rest relates to holiness and worship, not to lethargy or laziness.

- The Sabbath is a practical reminder to us of how we were saved—by faith (resting) in Jesus—and of God's promise of eternal life (rest) in him.

- The Sabbath principle was manifested in many of the Old Testament civil laws, especially the laws related to material stewardship and economics.

Action Points

- Why is rest so important? Have you ever neglected rest? If so, what were the consequences?

- What difference does Christ make for Sabbath-keeping? How is the principle of Sabbath-keeping different between the Old and New Testaments?

- Do you rest? How can you improve the way you rest in light of the Sabbath?

CHAPTER 4

Wealth and Poverty

Now that we've explored work and rest and their importance to issues of economics, stewardship, and living in the material world, we'll turn back to the themes of material wealth and poverty. These topics continue our discussion from the two previous chapters in the sense that mastering the disciplines of work and rest often results in wealth, while neglecting work or rest often leads to poverty. So let's look at wealth, along with giving and other related issues, and then move on to a consideration of poverty.

The Bible and Wealth

As we noted earlier, we must be careful about the categories we use to think and talk about wealth. We can be prone to mischaracterize wealth, viewing it as either "filthy lucre" (as the King James Version of the Bible translates 1 Timothy 3:3) or as a source of personal security and evidence of divine favor. There is no scriptural support for such polarized views of material possessions since the Bible neither condemns nor commends wealth apart from other factors, including means and motives. Indeed, God is not as concerned with how much wealth we possess so much as how we attain and steward our wealth.

Scripture teaches that God delights in the material prosperity of his followers as long as we properly recognize him as the source of all blessings (see Deut 28:11–13; Jas 1:17). Yet the Bible also cautions believers about the possession of wealth, as those with material possessions are vulnerable to wealth-related sins. Jesus taught in general on this topic in the parable of the Sower, noting that for some people, "the cares of the world and the deceitfulness of riches choke the word" (Matt 13:22). Since the measurement of wealth is relative, all of us need to heed Jesus' words of caution in this parable.

One specific category of sins about which the wealthy need to be especially cautious is a temptation to interact with the poor in a callous, sinful manner. For example, we learn from Jesus' narrative about Lazarus and the rich man that the wealthy sometimes ignore the poor. Lazarus the beggar, covered with sores "at [the rich man's] gate ... desired to be fed with what fell from the rich man's table" (Luke 16:20–21). Yet apparently Lazarus went unnoticed (or at least unhelped) by the rich man. Indeed, Jesus' narrative relates that the rich man's lack of benevolence was symptomatic of a spiritual condition that led to his being sent to Hades upon his death.

In the letter that bears his name, James mentions two sins similar to that of the rich man: marginalizing the poor in the church and oppressing the poor in the courts (see Jas 2:1–9). The poor lacked the social power of the rich, so it was easy for the wealthy to ignore them and to interact with them in a sinful manner, especially since there were usually few practical consequences for doing so. Immoral lending practices—another type of wealth-related sin— were prohibited under Old Testament law; these practices included making loans to the needy at exorbitant interest rates and seizing a debtor's means of production and protection (Deut 23:19–20; 24:12–13).

The wealthy are also prone to a second category of sin: putting trust in their riches rather than in God. In Psalm 52:7 David warns God's people, saying, "See the man who would not make God his refuge, but trusted in the abundance of his riches and sought refuge in his own destruction!" Indeed, wealth tends to tempt people toward luxurious living and self-indulgence (see Jas 5:5). Ironically, such excessive gratification often leads to a general sense of discontentment. The Preacher of Ecclesiastes noted this phenomenon, observing, "He who loves money will not be satisfied with money, nor he who loves wealth with his income" (Eccl 5:10). Ultimately, those who trust in their wealth as a source of security eventually reject spiritual truth and, without repentance, meet eternal destruction, like the Pharisees (see Luke 16:14–15; 1 Tim 6:9–10).

Wealth and Giving

Biblical warnings about wealth are primarily tied to an immoral withholding or giving of wealth. The admonitions just cited could be summed up: Don't fail to give to those in need and don't spend (give) immorally on oneself. In light of our fallen nature and our tendency to idolize wealth, these warnings are a helpful reminder. Yet, even if these admonitions are heeded, they raise several important questions about giving: What is the proper way to give? To whom should we give? How much should we give? In seeking answers to such questions, we'll turn our attention to tithing—the most common giving practice mentioned in Scripture.

The Hebrew term for "tithe," which literally means "tenth," is used 41 times in the Old Testament (32 times as a noun and 9 times as a verb). In the Old Testament, tithing was part of an economic system prescribed by God, which was part of a larger, theocratic (God-centered) political system. Tithing is mentioned only twice in the Old Testament apart from the context of the Jewish civil law (Gen 14:20; 28:22). In the governmental system prescribed by God, tithing was necessary for the healthy economic functioning of society, and all citizens of Israel were required to tithe. Perhaps the best modern parallel to the Old Testament tithe is property or income tax.

We may be surprised to learn that the historical books of the Bible describe the tithe as a joyous privilege among the people. For example, 2 Chronicles 31:5–6 reports,

> As soon as the command [to give] was spread abroad, the people of Israel gave in abundance ... they brought in abundantly the tithe of everything. And the people of Israel and Judah who lived in the cities of Judah also brought in

the tithe of cattle and sheep, and the tithe of
the dedicated things that had been dedicated to
the LORD their God, and laid them in heaps (see
also Neh 12:44; 13:12).

In the prophetic books, however, the tithe is presented as a
burden, as the practice was evidently neglected. Through
the prophet Amos, God confronted the Jews' idolatry and
sarcastically invited the people to indulge in their sins, saying, "Come to Bethel, and transgress; to Gilgal, and multiply
transgression; bring your sacrifices every morning, your
tithes every three days" (Amos 4:4). In a well-known passage from the book of Malachi, the people are accused of
robbing God of his tithes (Mal 3:8–10).

Many modern believers ask, "Are New Testament
Christians to follow the Old Testament tithe?" Some argue
for the practice of tithing, noting that it is simple to calcu-
late, it is biblical (in the sense of being found in the Bible),
it fosters local church commitment, and it allows for bud-
geting and advanced financial planning within the church.
Others argue against tithing, noting that the practice relies
on questionable Bible interpretation—that is, applying Old
Testament civil laws in the modern context. They say tithing tends to foster legalism when practiced, that it may be
unjust among those with differing incomes, and it has not
been taught or practiced among the majority of Christians
throughout church history. To address whether tithing is
applicable today, we'll need to study the topic further as it is
described in the Old Testament.

Tithing in the Old Testament

The concept of tithing is mentioned only twice in the Old Testament apart from the context of Jewish civil law. The first of these occurrences, and the first mention of tithing in Scripture, is in Genesis 14:20, where Abram gives a tenth of the spoils of war to Melchizedek, king of Salem. Contextually, this is the occasion when Abram rescued his nephew Lot, who had been taken captive in a war between several Canaanite kings. This tithe appears to have been a voluntary act of praise and thanksgiving in recognition of God's role in the battle victory. Note that Abram tithed on the spoils recovered from war—other people's property, not on his own property. Given that this tithe was not commanded by God, and was never repeated by Abram in the biblical narrative, it is difficult to apply this passage directly to a modern context.

The second mention of the tithe in the Old Testament, apart from civil laws, is in Genesis 28:22, where Jacob promises to give God a tenth of his increase if God would preserve his life and materially bless his journey. Contextually, this is the occasion when Jacob was fleeing from Esau on his way to seek refuge with Rebecca's family in Haran. As with the Abram narrative, it is difficult to apply Jacob's example to contemporary believers. Again, the tithe was not prescribed by God but appears to be Jacob's attempt to bargain with God during a time of uncertainty in his life—he sought to obtain divine favor while fleeing to a foreign land. It is also worth noting that there is no record of Jacob keeping this vow, although it is possible that he tithed on the occasion of erecting an altar when he returned to the promised land some 20 years later (Gen 33:18-20).

Apart from these two passages, all of the other mentions of the tithe in the Old Testament are in either civil law, a historical narrative concerning civil law, or a prophetic exhortation about observing civil law. In these passages, we see there were actually three separate tithes required within the Jewish civil law:

- The first and most often-cited tithe in the Old Testament is the Levitical tithe (see Lev 27:30-33; Num 18:21-32; Neh 10:37-38). This tithe, which is sometimes referred to as the firstfruits tithe, was an annual tithe to be given to the Levites since they had no land and thus no way to produce crops, raise livestock, or otherwise earn a living and provide for their families. This tithe was essentially the Levites' compensation for serving as priests. The law specified that the priests were to give 10 percent of the Levitical tithe to the high priest. Thus, no one (except the high priest) was exempt from paying this tithe. An interesting regulation relating to the Levitical tithe was the people's right to redeem a portion of their tithe by giving 120 percent of its value to the priests (see Lev 27:31).

- The second tithe specified in the civil law is the celebratory tithe, which is sometimes simply referred to as the second tithe (Deut 12:6-7, 11-12; 14:22-27).

As specified in Exodus 23:14–17, this tithe was to be set aside every year for use by Israelite worshipers as they traveled to and resided in Jerusalem to participate in the three mandatory annual religious celebrations at the temple. Moreover, the law noted that if extensive travel was required, produce of the field and flock could be sold and money brought to Jerusalem to finance the worshipers' own celebrations. As with the Levitical tithe, the people were to use a portion of the second tithe to meet the celebratory needs of the Levites.

- The third tithe in the civil law is the welfare tithe, which is also called the poor tithe (see Deut 14:28–29; 26:12). Scripture describes this tithe in Deuteronomy 14:28–29:

> At the end of every three years you shall bring out all the tithe of your produce in the same year and lay it up within your towns. ... The Levite ... and the sojourner, the fatherless, and the widow, who are within your towns, shall come and eat and be filled.

The law is clear that this tithe of benevolence was not intended for the sluggard, but for the truly poor—those whose poverty was truly a matter of life and death.

Accounting for these three tithes, it seems that the amount given each year was no less than 20 percent and no more than 30 percent of an Israelite's material earnings; the actual amount would depend on the collection of the welfare tithe in the third year. It's important to note that in the Sabbatical Year (see chapter 3), the Israelites would not offer any tithes, since there would have been no harvest and no firstfruits on such years. Over a seven-year cycle, then, the Israelites would have given according to this pattern: 20 percent, 20 percent, 30 percent, 20 percent, 20 percent, 30 percent, 0 percent. This averages out to a tithe of 20 percent every year over a seven-year cycle.

Would it be possible to apply these Old Testament civil tithing laws in our own context? It would be necessary to get both the amount and the application of the tithe correct in order to be biblical. But the lack of a modern-day theocracy and the specified use of the tithes—for supporting the Levitical priesthood, for personal expenses related to keeping certain Jewish ceremonial laws, and for benevolence—would make it all but impossible. And we must keep in mind that tithes were not used on things like temple operations and synagogue construction, since these were financed by a separate temple tax (see Exod 30:11–16; 2 Chr 24:6–10; Neh 10:32). So we are left with our initial questions regarding the proper giving of wealth in our own context. Fortunately, the New Testament provides related examples for us to examine.

Tithing in the New Testament

Despite the prevalence of tithing in the Old Testament, the practice is not mentioned in the New Testament by John, Paul, or Peter. In fact, the concept of tithing is mentioned only three times in the New Testament, with each reference being marginal in the context in which it occurs.

The first reference to tithing is in Matthew 23:23. Here, in a longer passage in which Jesus is confronting the scribes and Pharisees for their hypocrisy and legalism, he mentions the tithe (see Matt 23:1-36). In Matthew 23:23 Jesus says, "Woe to you, scribes and Pharisees, hypocrites! For you tithe mint and dill and cumin, and have neglected the weightier matters of the law: justice and mercy and faithfulness. These you ought to have done, without neglecting the others." Although this verse is a New Testament reference to tithing—made by Jesus himself—it is not an entirely commendable example of tithing, since Christ is confronting the religious leaders for their legalistic observation of the law.

The second mention of tithing in the New Testament is in Luke 18:11-12, within Jesus' parable of the Pharisee and the Tax Collector. In it, Jesus explains that a Pharisee and tax collector went to the temple to pray. The legalistic Pharisee prayed, "God, I thank you that I am not like other men, extortioners, unjust, adulterers, or even like this tax collector. I fast twice a week; I give tithes of all that I get" (Luke 18:11-12). Like the reference in Matthew 23:23, this citation does not exemplify a New Testament pattern for giving. As Jesus explains the meaning of this parable, the

Pharisee was not justified by his prayers or his tithing: "For everyone who exalts himself will be humbled, but the one who humbles himself will be exalted" (Luke 18:14).

The third and final mention of tithing in the New Testament occurs in Hebrews 7:1–10, where the author discusses the Old Testament character Melchizedek, king of Salem (mentioned earlier in this chapter). This passage reviews the narrative from Genesis 14:18–24, when Abram tithed of the spoils of war to Melchizedek upon returning safely from battle. So this passage in Hebrews is a retelling of an earlier account that included the practice of tithing, and it is peripheral to the author's argument in Hebrews about the superiority of Christ's priesthood over that of the Levites. As with the two references to tithing in the Gospels, there is little here to use for our own application.

Giving in the New Testament

With little New Testament support, it is difficult to apply Old Testament tithing laws in our own context. In fact, if we survey the New Testament, we'll find that it does not prescribe a formal method or fixed amount for believers' giving at all. The New Testament does, however, provide several examples and principles of giving that can guide us in our stewardship and giving. These principles ought to encourage many (if not most) Christians to give far more than 10 percent to kingdom work.

Two of the most important New Testament passages that address giving appear in Paul's letters to the Corinthian church. In 1 Corinthians 16:1–2, Paul writes, "Now concerning the collection for the saints: as I directed the churches of Galatia, so you also are to do. On the first day of every week, each of you is to put something aside and store it up, as he may prosper, so that there will be no collecting when I come." The second passage, which is too lengthy to quote here in its entirety, covers all of 2 Corinthians 8–9 (please, read it!). Using 1 Corinthians 16:2 as a rubric, and appealing to 2 Corinthians 8–9 for support, we can discern five principles of giving from Paul's instructions in these passages.

First, giving is to be periodic.
Paul writes to the Corinthian church, "On the first day of every week" (1 Cor 16:2). As we discussed in the previous chapter, there is ample biblical evidence that the early church met weekly, on Sunday (see John 20:26; Acts 20:7; Heb 4:9–10; Rev 1:10). Paul begins his instructions about giving, then, by noting that the Corinthian believers ought to give when they are gathered together on the first day of the week. Such giving would prevent a lack when funds were needed (see 2 Cor 8:10–14; 9:3–5). Of course, in our context, many believers are not compensated weekly; but even if one were paid on a biweekly or monthly basis, giving could still be periodic.

Second, giving is to be personal.
Paul continues his instructions to the Corinthian believers by writing, "[let] each of you" (1 Cor 16:2). Every Christian ought to give since generous giving is a personal response to receiving God's grace in and through Jesus Christ (see 2 Cor 8:1–2, 9; 9:15). God gave his only Son to atone for sin, to

reconcile us to him, and to provide eternal life to those who would repent and believe in Jesus. Christ came to earth so that we might become eternally rich through faith in him (2 Cor 8:9). God's grace toward us ought to be a motivation for giving—it is what Jesus appealed to in the parable of the Good Samaritan—and generous giving is a tangible expression of our love for God.

Third, giving must be planned.
Paul directed the Corinthians, "Put something aside and store it up" (1 Cor 16:2). Here Paul is calling for thought and intention in regard to giving. Note that Paul does not make an emotional plea by offering heart-wrenching stories. He does not appeal to guilt, nor does he endorse sporadic, impulsive giving of varying amounts. Rather, Paul calls for planned, thoughtful giving. In the book of 2 Corinthians, Paul also teaches intentional giving as he refers to giving with a willing mind (2 Cor 8:12) and references the gift that the Corinthians had previously promised (2 Cor 9:5).

Fourth, giving is to be proportionate.
As he continues his exhortation, Paul says each believer should give "as he may prosper" (1 Cor 16:2). Later, in 2 Corinthians 8:3, the apostle encourages believers to give "according to their means." In other words, each person was to give according to what he or she possessed. People with greater wealth could give more than those with less. In 2 Corinthians 8:12 Paul teaches the importance of having a heart that is ready and willing to give. He writes, "For if the readiness is there, it is acceptable according to what a

person has, not according to what he does not have." Paul does not want believers to give out of a sense of grudging obligation but proportionately, willingly, and cheerfully (see 2 Cor 9:7). Of course, giving in such a manner is only possible when one understands the gospel and loves God more than earthly possessions.

Fifth, giving is to be plentiful.
Paul concludes his instructions, "So that there will be no collecting when I come" (1 Cor 16:2). Generous giving is a sign of spiritual maturity and sincere love—and here, Paul challenges the Corinthian church to demonstrate the sincerity of their love for their brethren by giving to meet their material needs. In 2 Corinthians 8:7-8 the apostle encourages the church to abound in the grace of giving, just as they abound in faith, speech, and knowledge. Genuine love for God and growth in the Christian life will result in a mature, giving heart. Indeed, a heart dedicated to Christ cannot help but be generous toward God and his people, often (if not usually) leading us to voluntarily give far more than what was required under the Old Testament tithing regulations.

Communal Sharing

Another often-cited example of giving in the New Testament is the case of the early Christian converts in the book of Acts, who practiced a type of voluntary communal sharing. Acts 2:44-45 reads,

> And all who believed were together and had all things in common. And they were selling their

> possessions and belongings and distributing
> the proceeds to all, as any had need.

Additional details are recorded in Acts 4:32–35:

> Now the full number of those who believed
> were of one heart and soul, and no one said
> that any of the things that belonged to him
> was his own, but they had everything in com-
> mon. ... There was not a needy person among
> them, for as many as were owners of lands or
> houses sold them and brought the proceeds of
> what was sold and laid it at the apostles' feet,
> and it was distributed to each as any had need.

Some contemporary believers have suggested that this instance of communal sharing in the early church presents a model for Christians to follow. The communal sharing in Acts reflects the biblical ideal of provision for believers (see Psa 37:25–26) and embodies the principle of lending to those in need (see Deut 15:7–8; Luke 6:34). Yet we can see a number of reasons that the example of communal sharing in the early church is not a viable model for contemporary Christians.

First, in examining the context of communal sharing in the book of Acts, we see that it was an emergency aid effort sparked by the large number of foreign converts in Jerusalem when the church first began. Luke records that on the day of Pentecost, "There were added that day about three thousand souls. ... And the Lord added to their number day by day those who were being saved" (Acts 2:41, 47). In all likelihood, many of these new converts had not planned to lodge in Jerusalem longer than the few days of the Jewish feast. Consequently, there were many material needs among those in the early church who wanted to stay in Jerusalem to be taught by the apostles.

Second, we must note that the events in the book of Acts are narrative accounts, not prescriptive teachings. Although we can often learn from the stories and examples in the Bible, we must be careful about reaching doctrinal and moral conclusions from narratives, especially if such examples are unique, are not endorsed or repeated elsewhere in Scripture, or are contradicted by other examples or prescriptive teachings in the Bible. Indeed, there are many narratives in Scripture that even describe sinful events. We know this by evaluating them in light of the prescriptive teachings of Scripture. We must evaluate the communal sharing narrative in Acts by this same methodology before we can reach conclusions about its applicability for today.

Third, Bible scholars have noted that the tense of the Greek verbs used in the Acts narrative does not communicate permanent or completed actions. Rather, it indicates actions that are in progress or uncompleted. The New International Version of the Bible clearly communicates this truth in its translation of Acts 4:34-35, which reads, "From time to time those who owned land or houses sold them, brought money from the sales and put it at the apostles' feet." In other words, the early Christians did not all immediately liquidate their material resources and pool their money. Rather, as is often done now, when needs arose within the early church, those with material resources met the needs "from time to time."

Fourth, we must remember that the Bible offers other teachings and economic examples that differ from this narrative. For example, in his parable of the Talents, Jesus assigns a different number of talents to each individual (Matt 25:14–30). Paul freely labored among the churches to meet his own material needs rather than accept support from fellow believers (2 Thess 3:7–9), and he instructed the church to give freely to the poor, which would be nonsensical if all believers' assets were liquidated and held in common (see also 2 Cor 9:7). In his confrontation of Ananias about his land and money, Peter plainly taught that there was no burden on Christians to sell their assets (Acts 5:4).

So, in sum, the communal sharing example in Acts is not a mandate for Christians to liquidate their material possessions and pursue complete economic equality. Acts 4:32 says, "No one said that any of the things that belonged to him was his own." It does not say, "Everyone said that whatever belonged to anyone belonged to everyone." Indeed, the notion that Christians are to be economically equal rests on a faulty, static, zero-sum balance view of material resources—that is, the idea that economies cannot grow—which ignores the duty to and productivity of labor (you might want to review our discussion of work in chapter 2). We ought to expect a variation in material possessions in a world where God creates *individuals* with various gifts, talents, and abilities. So while the practice of the early church was not economic equality, the communal sharing narrative is a great example of promoting economic justice to meet the needs of the poor.

The Bible and Poverty

The Christian tradition has always stood in solidarity with the poor. James reminds his readers that caring for the poor is a mark of true religion (Jas 1:27). In a similar manner, John writes that a failure to care for the poor may be a sign of an unregenerate heart, as he rhetorically asks, "But if anyone has the world's goods and sees his brother in need, yet closes his heart against him, how does God's love abide in him?" (1 John 3:17). Indeed, those of us who follow Christ face high expectations in ministering to the poor. Jesus teaches that caring for the poor is the same as caring for God himself (Matt 25:31–40), while neglecting the poor is an offense to God (Matt 25:41–46). Proverbs teaches these same truths, saying, "Whoever oppresses a poor man insults his Maker. ... Whoever is generous to the poor lends to the LORD" (Prov 14:31; 19:17).

As we noted in the first chapter, ministering to the poor can be a very challenging task since the measurement of poverty is relative and the causes are varied. Even in Scripture, the discussion of poverty is paradoxical at points. For instance, God's stated ideal is clearly that "there will be no poor among you" (Deut 15:4). Yet, as we discussed earlier, Jesus voluntarily adopted a life of poverty and taught, "Blessed are you who are poor" (Luke 6:20). As we seek to minister to the poor in a biblically faithful way, these tensions highlight how important it is for us to answer pressing contextual questions: Is the poverty in view voluntary or involuntary? Is the poverty in question the result of personal sin, public injustice, or some other cause? Does the situation call for immediate aid or long-term development?

The Causes of Poverty

One way we can gain a proper foundational perspective on ministry to the poor is by examining the causes of poverty. Indeed, identifying the cause(s) of poverty in any given context can help us understand how best to minister to the poor, if ministry is called for. As we'll discover during our discussion, the roots of poverty fall into three general categories. But it is important to note that the causes of poverty in a given context are usually mixed and self-aggravating. This is one of the many reasons why ministry to the poor can be complex and why it often (if not, usually) requires a personal, long-term commitment.

The first category of causes of poverty is personal sin. Scripture often mentions moral failures that lead to poverty. For example, the Bible warns about poverty as a result of laziness or idleness (see Prov 6:10–11; 10:4; 19:15; 1 Thess 5:14). Likewise, Proverbs warns about the effects of a poor work ethic (see Prov 14:23), and Paul teaches that those who will not work should not be insulated from the effects of their sin—namely, they should not be allowed to eat (2 Thess 3:10).

Scripture cites other moral failures as cause for poverty, including a lack of self-discipline, stubbornness, drunkenness, and gluttony (see Prov 13:18; 23:21). Jesus called out these sins in his parable of the Prodigal Son, describing how the wayward younger brother made his way into poverty (Luke 15:11–16). Poverty can stem from other personal sins, including greed, expensive tastes, dishonesty, and frivolous pursuits. For example, Proverbs warns us, "Whoever loves pleasure will be a poor man; he who loves wine and oil will not be rich. ... He who follows worthless pursuits will have plenty of poverty" (Prov 21:17; 28:19; see also 1 Tim 6:9–10).

Natural evil is the second category of causes of poverty. Simply defined, natural evil consists of things such as natural disasters (earthquakes, tornadoes, tsunamis, floods, droughts, and other "acts of God"), diseases, genetic defects, injuries, and death. Natural evil is not directly caused by a person's own actions or actions against them by another person. Rather, this type of evil is a part of the fallen created order and, as such, involves material forces beyond human control. Natural evil can lead to poverty when it causes a loss of material goods, the death of a family provider, or a disease or physical infirmity that prevents a person from labor and production (see Mark 5:25–26; Luke 18:35).

A third category of causes of poverty is oppression by others. Unlike natural evil, this type of poverty can be prevented; thus, Scripture frequently warns against oppressing others. Examples of oppression that cause poverty include common theft (Psa 12:5), delayed wages (Lev 19:13; Deut 24:15; 1 Tim 5:18), excessive taxation (2 Chr 10:1–19), biased justice systems (Lev 19:15), and exorbitant interest rates on loans to the needy (Exod 22:25–27). Many of these types of oppression are systematic or institutionalized, or become so over time; thus, they tend to affect larger groups of people than do individual sins. Perhaps this is why the Lord promises to defend those who fall prey to this type of oppression and exhorts us to do the same (Psa 146:9; Isa 1:17).

Ministering to the Poor

Given the prevalence of poverty in our fallen world and its many origins, how can we best minister to the poor? Of course, we cannot offer a comprehensive answer to such a broad question, not when each instance of poverty is unique and needs to be addressed individually. Yet we can follow several general principles in any context of poverty—principles that will allow us to work toward biblically faithful, individual solutions.

First, we must discern if the situation calls for aid or development. An aid-based model is one in which resources are distributed indiscriminately in light of a pressing material need. We see this type of relief most often in emergency situations where poverty has been caused by natural evil, such as a medical emergency, a natural disaster, or another unanticipated event. Examples of such aid include temporary shelter in the aftermath of a hurricane or meals for a family while a loved one is hospitalized. In emergency situations such as these, an aid-based model of relief is appropriate and helpful in addressing and/or preventing poverty. This is the type of aid provided in the example of communal sharing found in Acts that was discussed earlier.

However, an aid-based model of poverty relief can cause problems and even prolong poverty if we handle it improperly. In some cases, when we give aid indiscriminately and long term, beneficiaries can become dependent on it and even stop working to meet their own needs. The aid-based model of poverty relief can cause the related problem of enabling sin. If we help those who are impoverished because of their sin, our efforts can insulate them from the effects of their sin, thus robbing them of a natural motivation for repentance. A final problem with aid-based models of poverty relief is that they have historically tended to propagate relief organizations. While this is not problematic in itself, organizations that make up the so-called "poverty industry" have a conflict of interest in regard to the existence and alleviation of poverty. Of course, this is not to say that all (or any) relief organizations are evil, but it is a caveat that if an aid-based model of poverty relief is misapplied, it places certain relief organizations into a situation of possible codependence.

In such cases, the alternative developmental model can be far more effective. Under this paradigm, we can attempt to affect poverty in ways that allow for long-term productivity. Such an approach is not appropriate in emergency situations, but is usually the best course of action when poverty is caused by personal sin or oppression. Examples of developmental relief include providing job-skills training to an impoverished community, working to change unjust civil laws designed to keep new businesses out of the marketplace, laboring on behalf of a minority neighborhood to ensure residents have access to law enforcement, or reaching out with the gospel (in conjunction with discipleship and long-term accountability) to help individuals overcome their poverty-causing sins.

By turning to a developmental model of aid, we seek to endorse and protect the connection between work and production. But doing so requires us to make a longer-term commitment and have more personal interaction than in aid-based relief, so such efforts are usually more difficult to implement and sustain. While some cases undoubtedly call for short-term intervention, our efforts to help transition the poor from impoverishment to productivity are arguably more important, even if they are more difficult. Indeed, successful ministry to the poor should not be measured by how much we give away, but by how many people we can help overcome and remain out of poverty. Developmental efforts should cause us to question our motives. In John 12:6–8, Jesus confronts Judas Iscariot, who suggested that the nard ointment Mary brought to anoint Jesus should be sold and the money given to the poor. Judas' concern was not for the poor but for himself—he was in charge of the moneybag and helped himself to its contents. If we are seeking some profit or glory from helping the poor, we will not do the hard work of developmental relief.

Discernment is a second principle to keep in mind as we minister to the poor. An earlier generation coined the phrases "deserving poor" and "undeserving poor" as reminders that we must seek to discern the cause(s) of the poverty as well as the character of those who are impoverished. When we encounter those who are poor due to natural evil or oppression, we should naturally consider them to be the deserving poor and strive to provide them with resources to alleviate their poverty. But when we seek to help those who are poor because of personal sin, we ought to offer aid only if they are repentant and willing to participate in a developmental model of relief. Although it's difficult to discern the root of poverty and the character of the impoverished, we must exercise discernment in ministering to the poor.

A final principle we should consider when caring for the poor is the concept of moral proximity, which is sometimes called the principle of proximate obligation. This concept teaches that poverty is best addressed and alleviated by those closest to the situation. Such individuals or groups will usually have the best understanding of the situation and the people involved. Shades of this concept can be seen in Scripture when we are encouraged to care for our own families (1 Tim 5:4, 8), for our descendants (Prov 13:22), for the members of the church (Rom 12:13), for those in the community (Gal 6:10), and for the whole world (Matt 28:19-20). Our efforts to address poverty will be most effective in this order.

Social Justice

Before concluding our discussion of poverty, let's briefly discuss the concept of social justice, since the discussion of one often leads to discussion of the other. Today's Christians have demonstrated a growing interest in establishing justice in society—a good thing, as long as we define justice biblically. Indeed, justice is a fundamental aspect of God's character (see Deut 10:17–18; Jer 9:24), and the Lord requires justice of his followers (Mic 6:8). The Bible specifically instructs believers to apply justice in both legal (Deut 16:18; Jer 21:12) and economic matters (Lev 19:36). Scripture depicts those who ignore or pervert justice as being wicked (Prov 19:28; Luke 11:42) and teaches that social injustice is the result of sin.

Even so, we must define justice biblically. Secularists and some Christians err in equating social justice with equality of material resources. As we've already noted, Scripture does not indicate a preference for any specific material status, nor does it call for all people to have equal resources. Rather, the Bible describes a just society as one that treats all people with objectivity and dignity (see Lev 19:15; 24:22; Isa 1:17). The aim of social justice, then, is to achieve and to maintain impartiality, not material equality of individuals or uniformity of outcomes. As Christians seek social justice, then, we should focus on three goals: (1) an unprejudiced evaluation of individuals as image-bearers of God; (2) an impartial application of civil laws that embody the unchanging moral law of God, and (3) a proportional connection between actions and outcomes, especially in legal and economic matters.

Heading Forward

Having surveyed biblical teachings on wealth and poverty in this chapter, we'll head toward the conclusion of our study of the material realm in the next chapter by looking more closely at the created order itself. As we'll see, the material world is not just the realm in which we labor and rest as well as experience wealth and poverty. Indeed, it is our present and future home—and we must steward it properly.

Summary

- God is not as concerned with how much wealth we possess as he is with how we attain and steward our wealth.

- Whereas the Old Testament required the Israelites to give by means of the tithe, the New Testament does not prescribe a formal method or fixed amount for believers' giving.

- The idea that Christians are to be economically equal ultimately ignores the duty to work and the productivity of labor.

- Identifying the cause(s) of poverty is essential for knowing how to best minister to the poor.

- The aim of social justice is to achieve and to maintain impartiality, not material equality of individuals or uniformity of outcomes.

Action Points

- What biblical principles should guide us in earning and spending wealth?

- Have you ever struggled with embarrassment for not having enough money? Guilt for having too much money? What is Jesus' attitude toward the amount of money we have?

- How do you obey Jesus in caring for the poor?

CHAPTER 5

Creation and Stewardship

We've discussed many topics related to living in the material world. As we draw closer to the end of our study, it may be helpful for us to take a step back so we can gain a panoramic view of this realm in which we labor, rest, and find ourselves in a state of either relative wealth or poverty—that is, in the created order. Taking a wide-angle view, so to speak, of the created order may help us to gain a better perspective on the specifics of how we are to relate to each other, how to properly interact with creation, and how we can best serve God as stewards within and over the material world. To use another camera metaphor, in this chapter, we'll take a snapshot of the forest so we can better understand the trees within it.

Caring for Creation

Why should Christians care about the creation? Isn't the material world going to burn up one day anyway? If our citizenship is in heaven, why should we care about the earth? We need to ask and answer these types of inquiries in our study of the material world. In the opening chapter, we briefly addressed some foundational questions related to caring for the material realm, but additional observations will help us better answer these types of questions as we seek to develop a biblical perspective on living in (and caring for) the material world for the common good.

First, Christianity is a comprehensive worldview, not a philosophy disconnected from everyday life. As such, Christianity and the gospel message should affect every area of our existence, including the salvation of souls, the reformation of morals, and the restoration of the material world. Indeed, this is a foundational premise of this book. "Restoring all the things," to use Peter's phrase from Acts 3:21, will not be finally and completely accomplished until the return of Christ, yet our desire to be faithful stewards should motivate us to interact with this fallen world in light of what it will one day be. Doing so is part of our labor as image-bearers of God. In fact, as Genesis 1–2 reveals, the earth was not designed to function properly apart from human care. God made the earth to be stewarded by humanity.

Second, the created order is where we dwell—where we labor and rest—and it is the sphere of God's redemptive activities. We should take an active interest in caring for it. Along these lines the psalmist wrote, "Great are the works of the LORD, studied by all who delight in them" (Psa 111:2). In Scripture, this pattern of interest in the material world is manifest among the people of God. For example, 1 Kings 4:33 notes, "[Solomon] spoke of trees, from the cedar that is in Lebanon to the hyssop that grows out of the wall.

He spoke also of beasts, and of birds, and of reptiles, and of fish." Similarly, during his reign, David appointed forestry and agricultural officials throughout Israel (1 Chr 27:27-28). And it is said that godly King Uzziah "loved the soil" (2 Chr 26:10). Such an interest in God's creation ought to be prevalent among and displayed by God's people—a lack of interest in the material world is profoundly unbiblical.

We should also be motivated to engage with and care for creation knowing that, in so doing, we can gain knowledge of God. Indeed, God began to reveal himself to us in the context of creation (Gen 1-2), and Scripture further testifies to the understanding of God available to us through the material world (see Psa 19:1-6; 104; Rom 1:19-20). Paul teaches that this knowledge can be "clearly perceived" (Rom 1:20) since God made the world and those in it. Since all that God does reflects his character and communicates his essence, creation necessarily reveals its creator. More specifically, though, Scripture provides examples of the Lord appealing to his own work in the material world as a means of revealing himself to his people. Perhaps the best example of this is God's response to Job's questions about his suffering: in this dialogue, God gives a detailed narrative about his own creative genius (see Job 38:1-41:34).

Finally, our care for creation, pursued in a biblical manner, both validates and displays the gospel message. Just as many of Jesus' miracles communicated the triumph of the gospel over sin-tainted creation, so our care for the material world and those in it can communicate the same message—albeit in a less powerful and less comprehensive way. Jesus healed the sick; we can care for them. Jesus created food; we can prepare and distribute it. Jesus calmed the storm; we can steward the environment. Furthermore, as with all other areas of Christian living, our actions to bring the gospel to bear upon the fallen material world will answer many of Christianity's detractors and may prove attractive to the watching world.

Worldviews and Creation

The multitude of competing worldviews within any given culture can make it difficult to cultivate a Christian view of creation. Believers can be confused by this multiplicity of views, which can lead to an inconsistent view of the material world. Yet every coherent worldview includes a perspective on the material world as well as a moral framework that defines how we should interact with the creation. While each culture comprises many different religions, philosophies, and ideologies, for the sake of simplicity, we'll focus now on the three main worldviews of our contemporary culture. We'll cover each position's view of God, humanity, and the created order. We'll also evaluate each worldview from a Christian perspective as we build a biblical case for creation care and stewardship.

Materialism

In modern Western culture, the most prevalent worldview is materialism, also called secular humanism. This is the perspective of the world that you'll find among atheists, agnostics, and many nominal Christians as well as others without a formal or defined religion. The materialist view of God is quite simple: God does not exist, at least not in a tangible way. Secular humanists who do believe in the existence of God would affirm that God is completely transcendent—that is, God is absent or divorced from the created order, equivalent to an absentee landlord. Thus, from an accountability standpoint, for secular humanists, moral interaction with the material world is not an entirely relevant issue.

The materialist view of mankind is a corollary to its view of God. In short, secular humanism affirms that by evolution, design, or default, humanity is lord of the universe. Moreover, at the heart of secular humanism is a supreme confidence in humanity to solve the problems of the world via education and technology. This can clearly be seen in the 1973 *Humanist Manifesto II*, which reads,

> Using technology wisely, we can control our environment, conquer poverty, markedly reduce disease, extend our life-span, significantly modify our behavior, alter the course of human evolution and cultural development, unlock vast new powers, and provide humankind with unparalleled opportunity for achieving an abundant and meaningful life.[1]

---

1. The American Humanist Association, "Humanist Manifesto II," 1973, http://http://americanhumanist.org/humanism/humanist_manifesto_ii.

Of course, one's interpretation of history in the decades since the appearance of the *Humanist Manifesto II* will influence one's conclusions regarding the statement's optimistic view of mankind's potential.

Secular humanists view the material world as mechanical and eternal (or, at least, as having evolved out of preexistent eternal matter). Materialists understand the created order to operate according to fixed natural laws. Thus, God does not intervene in the material world—either because he does not exist, lacks power or knowledge to intervene, or is altogether absent and unconcerned. Secular humanism recognizes that nature can be appreciated for its sense of beauty as defined by humanity, yet this ideology teaches that the created order has no inherent value other than to meet human needs. This view, then, is an anthropocentric view, as it understands the material world to have been formed *ex materia* (out of matter). Within secular humanism, the proper use and misuse of the material world is measured solely by self-interest and self-preservation. Consequently, materialist views of labor, rest, wealth, poverty, and the like tend to be completely pragmatic and utilitarian.

From a Christian perspective there are many problems with a secular humanistic worldview. Obviously, this position has a faulty view of God, even denying his existence or overemphasizing his transcendence. A by-product of materialism's denial of God's power is that humanity assumes the vacated role of God within this worldview. Yet, historically speaking, humanity's assumption of God's authority has proven to be problematic at best. Indeed, humankind seems ill suited to handle the sovereignty bestowed upon them by this worldview. Consequently, within this system the natural world ceases to be an environment to be properly stewarded under God's authority and is reduced to a resource to be consumed by humanity. Secular humanism, then, is both personally unfulfilling and destructive to the created order, for it robs people of their dignity and the creation of its inherent value.

Panentheism

A second worldview that is popular in the contemporary culture is panentheism. This position, or a hybrid version of it, is the view held by advocates of many Eastern religions, including Hinduism, Buddhism, Taoism, and the New Age movement. While there are many different nuances among these religious systems that extend well beyond the scope of this chapter, a commonality related to their view of God is their belief in God's immanent yet nonpersonal nature. To elaborate, a panentheistic view of God could be summarized as "all is one" or "all is God." This worldview holds that there is only one substance in the universe, which is God. Therefore, all things are an emanation of God; however, the God of panentheism is unknowable in a personal way.

A panentheistic view of man complements the view of God within this worldview. As could be expected, given panentheism's "all is one" mentality, this position understands humankind to be of the same fundamental essence as the rest of the created order. Consequently, this worldview understands mankind to be divine—but no more divine than the rest of the material world. Given the divine nature of the entire created order, panentheism teaches that humanity should not exercise dominion over the material world nor even attempt to steward it, for to do so would be imperialistic. Rather, this worldview holds that human beings are to mutually serve the created order as they would a brother or sister who needed care or guidance. They are to strive for what can be called "biological egalitarianism"—that is, an equality between human beings and the material world—as they seek to harmonize themselves with nature.

By extension, panentheism understands the material world to be divine and one with God (and, thus, also with human beings). This is ultimately a biocentric view of the created order that teaches the material world was created *ex deo* (out of God). Often, panentheists will refer to the material world as a living organism, as they ascribe human characteristics to it. Examples include calling the world "Mother Earth," referring to environmental destruction as "raping" the earth, and speaking of mankind and wildlife as being "brothers and sisters" who are all part of the same "circle of life." The impact of panentheism in the culture can be seen in the common use of such terminology in casual conversations about the material world, as well as in contemporary forms of media.

From a Christian perspective, there are many problems with panentheism. Most importantly, this worldview so overemphasizes God's immanence, while minimizing his personality, that it confuses the Creator with the creation. In fact, God as represented by panentheism cannot really be

God at all—at least not in the Christian understanding of the concept; such a God would be contingent, since the created order can be destroyed. At the same time, this worldview devalues humanity, by denying its majesty and making human beings equal to the material world. Furthermore, as history has shown, this position will ultimately prove to be self-destructive, for if God does not exist in a personal way, and mankind has no inherent value, there is no reason why people should worship God, respect one another, or conserve the creation.

Christian Theism

A final worldview in contemporary culture—indeed, the perspective from which this book is written—is Christian theism. This position teaches that God is transcendent in that he created the material world and exists apart from it (see Acts 17:24–25), yet God is immanent in that he indwells believers, continually sustains the creation, and is sovereign over all things (see Rev 4:11). Christian theism holds that while God is not identical with the creation (contra panentheism), he is nevertheless intimately concerned with and exercises authority over the entire material world (contra secular humanism). In this sense, Christian theism affirms a balance between God's immanence and transcendence, while affirming his personal nature.

As has been discussed in the preceding chapters, Christian theism teaches that human beings are made in God's image. While human beings are not the focal point of history (see Eph 1:10), Scripture nevertheless testifies that humanity is the crown of God's creation, being made "a little lower than the heavenly beings and crowned ... with glory and honor" (Psa 8:5). As we've previously discussed, one of the ways humanity functionally bears God's image is by exercising dominion over the created order and by procreating in order to fill the material world with other image-bearers of God. Such labor is expected of us by God and is ultimately a matter of stewardship.

Christian theism teaches that the material world was created *ex nihilo* (out of nothing) and that it is contingent upon God. As such, this position's view of the created order is theocentric. This worldview teaches that God made the material world for his own glory (see Col 1:16) and that the creation bears witness to and reflects the Creator (see Psa 19:1–4). Further, Christian theism teaches that the material world, which was made to be stewarded by mankind, currently labors under a curse because of humanity's sin. However, as Paul wrote, one day "the creation itself will be set free from its bondage to corruption and obtain the freedom of the glory of the children of God" (Rom 8:21). Indeed, when Christ returns, the heavens and earth will be renewed, and God and man will dwell together in harmony for eternity.

Creation and the Fall

In our attempt to gain a better perspective of the material world, it will be helpful to look further into the biblical teaching on creation and the fall as well as humanity's role as a steward of the material world. Indeed, a large part of the creation narrative details human beings' role as stewards of the created order. While we briefly discussed this idea in our study of work in chapter 3, more can be said in relation to creation and stewardship.

God made the world good. Indeed, the declaration "and it was good" is a mantra that resounds throughout the creation week described in Genesis 1. As we've already discussed, God made human beings and placed them in the good world that he had made. The fact that humanity's stewarding of the material world is the only purpose mentioned in the divine deliberation about creating human beings indicates that our stewardship of the created order is fundamental to human existence (see Gen 1:26). Upon their creation, God instructed Adam and Eve to have dominion over the material world and to procreate. We see these duties born out in Adam's tending of the garden of Eden, in his naming of the animals, and in the later arrival of their offspring as described in Genesis 4–5. It is also noteworthy in the creation story that Adam and Even were given permission to eat of the plants, and mankind was later allowed to partake of the animals (Gen 1:29–30; 2:9; 9:3). Such consumption indicates the place of human beings within and over the material world.

The fall of humanity was ultimately about the rejection of God's authority and the attempt to usurp God's place. As with all sin, so humanity's rejection of God in the garden of Eden was foolish and resulted in divine judgment. However, God's judgment upon people for their sin was not an uncontrolled outburst of wrath, but a righteous decree of justice that included a declaration that the material world would no longer operate smoothly according to its creational design. In part, the penalty for the fall entailed recognition that people would be sinful in their dealings with the created order and would be disobedient in regard to their divinely assigned roles of stewardship and procreation. More specifically, in judging humanity for its sin, God allowed people to pursue their own sin, frustrated people's labor, made childbirth painful, and made the cultivation of the ground difficult.

The practical effects of the fall upon the created order are cited and illustrated repeatedly throughout Scripture. These include physical death (Gen 2:17), animals being afraid of people (Gen 9:2), thorns and thistles (Gen 3:18), pain in childbirth (Gen 3:16), droughts (Lev 26:18-20), famines (1 Kgs 8:37-40), physical illnesses (Lev 26:21), the destruction caused by moths and rust (Matt 6:19), floods (Gen 7:1-8:19), and plagues (Lev 26:25). In short, as the psalmist writes, because of humanity's sin and the curse upon the created order, the material world "will all wear out like a garment" (Psa 102:26). In a small way, this creational decay allows humanity to experience life without God—a path that human beings chose for themselves in the fall—in hope that people will repent and return to God (see Rom 8:20).

Redemption and Restoration

Despite the divine curse upon the material world, God still continues to superintend and to provide for the created order. For example, the Bible teaches that God waters the ground, even where no one lives (Job 38:26); God knows the names of all the stars (Psa 147:4); God creates the wind and the darkness (Amos 4:13); God causes rain, clouds, thunder, ice, and snow (Job 37:1–13); God clothes the grass of the field (Matt 6:30); God limits the borders of the ocean (Psa 104:9); God feeds the birds of the air (Matt 6:26); God cares for livestock (Psa 104:11); and God causes the grass to grow (Psa 104:14). It is clear that while fallen people will continue to mistreat the earth (Isa 24:5), humanity will not succeed in completely destroying the earth (2 Pet 3:7), for God cares for the world that he made—even in its present fallen state.

God also continues to provide for and to meet the material needs of fallen humanity. Indeed, one of the first acts of God after the fall was to provide clothing for Adam and Eve (Gen 3:21). Another example of such postfall material provision is God's care for the Israelites during the exodus event. Despite their continual sin and apostasy during the exodus, God provided for his people, giving them manna (Exod 16:14–36), water (Exod 15:25; 17:1–7; Num 20:8–11), and even meat to eat (Exod 16:1–13; Num 11:31–32). Further, in the Gospels, Jesus instructs believers not to worry about their needs in the material world:

> Therefore do not be anxious, saying, "What shall we eat?" or "What shall we drink?" or "What shall we wear?" For the Gentiles seek after all these things, and your heavenly Father knows that you need them all. But seek first the

> kingdom of God and his righteousness, and all
> these things will be added to you (Matt 6:31–33).

As we've noted several times in the preceding discussion, God's care for the material world ultimately extends to all things. Writing about the plan of God and the effect of the gospel, Paul taught that in "the fullness of time ... [God will] unite all things in him, things in heaven and things on earth" (Eph 1:10; see also Col 1:15–20). Indeed, the scope of God's plan of redemption includes the salvation of humanity and the purging of the entire created order of the effects of sin. Scripture teaches that Christ did not come to finally remove people from the world but to deliver us from sin so that we can glorify God in this world and labor to re-create all things—a project that will only be fully and permanently accomplished by God at Jesus' return. The effect of the gospel is no less comprehensive than the effect of the fall.

Scripture calls this re-created material world the new heavens and new earth, which will appear at the consummation of the ages (see 2 Pet 3:12–13; Rev 21:1–22:5). As we observed in chapter 3, the term used for "new" in these passages means "new in nature or in quality," not "new in essence or being." In a sense, then, the re-creation of the material world is analogous to the process of individual salvation: Just as a believer gains new life but is still the same person, so the material world will be made new, not re-created from scratch. Recall we noted earlier Peter's allusion to Noah's flood—which was a prototype of this, for the flood led to the re-creation of the world, not its ultimate destruction (see 2 Pet 3:1–7). Indeed, it is more glorifying to God to restore than to annihilate the created order. Along these lines, note Jesus' teaching about the future of believers in the Sermon on the Mount: "Blessed are the meek, for they shall inherit the earth" (Matt 5:5; see also Psa 37:11).

There are not many facts about the new heavens and new earth in Scripture; however, there are several details worth considering. For instance, the Bible speaks of a renewed earth, free from the effects of the curse of sin. Although the present creation will "wear out like a garment," God "will change them like a robe" (Psa 102:26; see also Isa 55:12–13). Details of this change include the desert blooming (Isa 35:1–2, 6–7), water flowing as a river from the temple in Jerusalem into the Dead Sea in order to restore it (Ezek 47:1–12), and the presence of new wine and milk (Joel 3:18; Amos 9:13–15), trees and vineyards (Isa 65:21; Rev 22:1–2), and precious stones (Rev 21:18–21). In addition, the new heavens and new earth will include restored animals (Isa 11:6–8; 65:25). Moreover, in the final state, man will exercise proper dominion over the created order in fulfillment of God's creational design (Hos 2:18).

Heading Forward

With this larger perspective on the material world in view, including its ultimate destiny, we are better positioned to steward the creation well. As we work and rest, experience wealth and poverty, and interact with our fellow image-bearers within the created order, we need to draw upon our knowledge of "the end of the story" as a motivation to properly bring the gospel to bear upon the material aspects of our lives. Let Peter's exhortation to the first-century Christians be an encouragement to you: Since the day of the Lord's return to the material world is imminent, "what sort of people ought you to be in lives of holiness and godliness, waiting for and hastening the coming of the day of God" (2 Pet 3:11–12).

Summary

- Believers should care for the material creation, for the gospel is no less comprehensive than the fall. Jesus' reign extends to the restoration of all things.

- Worldviews other than Christian theism have resulted in destructive views of creation and poor stewardship of the material world.

- Like humanity, the creation currently labors under the curse of sin, yet it will eventually be set free from its bondage to corruption.

- The curse upon the created order was not an outburst of divine wrath, but an expression of God's love as he allows people to experience the results of their sin in hopes of their repentance.

- Jesus did not come to finally remove people from the world but to deliver us from sin so that we can glorify God in this world and labor to re-create all things.

Action Points

- How does your view of the future impact the way you treat the material creation right now?

- Have you ever avoided caring for creation out of fear of being associated with a worldview different than your own?

- How can you better care for creation? What practical steps can you take to align your actions with your faith?

CHAPTER 6

Conclusions

We've come a long way in this book, covering a wide range of topics relating to the material world. As we conclude our study, let's take a closer look at two of Jesus' parables, each of which contains foundational principles from our exploration. Reviewing these parables will help us as we seek to process the material we've covered and to live in the material world for the common good.

The Parable of the Talents

The parable of the Talents is recorded in Matthew 25:14–30. Although this passage is too lengthy to quote here, when we read it, it's clear that Jesus is teaching about life in the kingdom of heaven, for he begins the story by saying, "[The kingdom of heaven] will be like" (Matt 25:14). More specifically, though, the parable of the Talents warns us about wasting resources and opportunities as we engage in kingdom work within the material world. If you're not familiar with the parable, please take time to read it now, before we make three observations from this parable about living in the material world.

First, let's note that not everyone in the material world begins with the same amount of resources, and that's fine. Jesus does not assign the same number of talents to each character in the parable. In fact, the amount each man receives is dramatically different: One servant receives five talents, the next gets two talents, and the last receives only one talent. Real-world experience teaches us that this is exactly what the material realm is like. The resources with which we begin life and those we steward throughout life vary depending on our abilities, personality, family, friends, era, country, and a host of other factors. Even so, neither the parable of the Talents nor any other passage of Scripture presents this inequality of talents as being problematic or unjust per se.

Second, note that God holds everyone to the same standard—regardless of how many material resources they have been given to steward. In Jesus' parable, the man who labored to turn his five talents into ten, as well as the man who turned his two talents into four, received the same exact commendation from the master: "Well done, good and faithful servant. You have been faithful over a little; I will set you over much. Enter into the joy of your master" (Matt 25:21, 23). The man who didn't truly know the master, who squandered his opportunities and his master's resources, was not chastised for possessing only one initial talent. Rather, the master condemned him for his lack of effort and poor stewardship. We need to focus on properly stewarding that with which God has entrusted us in the material world and not worry that someone else may have begun life with—or may currently possess—more or less than us.

Third, let's look at what guided each servant in stewarding his given talents: his knowledge of and relationship with the master. The first two servants understood their role as stewards who were accountable for their actions when their master returned. In fact, they seem happy to give an account of their stewardship upon his return. The last servant clearly did not know his master, believing him to be "a hard man" (Matt 25:24), worthy of fear, who regularly acted unjustly in his dealings with others. Upon his return, the master told this servant that even such a misperception should have guided him to a different course of action; but no matter his master's true character, the servant was "wicked and slothful" (Matt 25:26). So it is with us: As our knowledge of God matures, we will learn to take right actions in the material world.

The Parable of the Good Samaritan

In Luke 10:29–37 Jesus tells the parable of the Good Samaritan in response to an inquiry about salvation from a self-righteous lawyer (Luke 10:25–28) wanting to know, "Who is my neighbor?" (Luke 10:29). If you aren't familiar with this parable, I encourage you to take a moment to read it. Within this parable, the injured Jew on the side of the road represents the lawyer, the Samaritan represents God, and the unmerited help provided is a picture of salvation. In essence, the lawyer asked Christ, "Who is my neighbor?"

and Jesus responded by asking, "Who has been neighbor to you?" Through this parable, Jesus taught the lawyer that salvation is by grace alone, not by works—and he provided the ultimate answer to the lawyer's initial question about salvation. Once we have been saved, when it comes to neighborly interaction, our lives should abound with good works. Indeed, as we see from Jesus' words in the Lord's Prayer, an understanding of God's forgiveness should inform all of our works (Matt 6:12-15; see also Matt 5:9-15). Grace should motivate our every action and interaction with the material world and those in it.

As we labor in our vocations, we need to be consciously dependent on grace, not motivated by greed. As we steward our wealth and give to our churches, we need to be motivated by grace, not by guilt. As we interact with the poor, we need to be driven by grace, not by pity. As we interact with the created order, we need to be aware of God's preserving grace, not overwhelmed by the effects of sin on the created order. Like the lawyer in Jesus' parable, we can be tempted toward self-righteousness in our actions, self-deception in our thoughts, and self-sufficiency with our resources. But when we shift our focus away from ourselves, we realize that only through God's provision and grace, made possible through the cross, can we live in the material world for the common good.

I n an attempt to make this book more readable, I have pur-
posely not cited any other works. There are, however, a
number of books that have shaped my thinking on material
world–related issues over the years. I would commend the
following works to readers who are interested in further ex-
ploring the topics covered in this text.

Bradley, Anne R., and Arthur W. Lindsley, eds. *For the Least of These:
A Biblical Answer to Poverty*. Grand Rapids: Zondervan, 2015.
An edited volume of articles related to wealth creation and
poverty alleviation written by conservative theologians and
economists. Topics range from biblical exegesis on relevant
passages to commentary on markets, justice, and the economy.

Fikkert, Brian, and Steve Corbett. *When Helping Hurts: Alleviating
Poverty without Hurting the Poor and Yourself*. Chicago: Moody,
2009. Widely recognized as one of the best books on a developmental model of poverty relief. Contains both foundational
teachings from Scripture and practical application. Topics addressed range from models of poverty relief to missions work.

Grudem, Wayne. *Business for the Glory of God: The Bible's Teaching on
the Moral Goodness of Business*. Wheaton, IL: Crossway, 2003.
A brief explanation of the impact of the gospel upon the workplace. Also contains a biblical theology of work that addresses

topics such as productivity, profit, and borrowing and lending, among other subjects.

Grudem, Wayne, and Barry Asmus. *The Poverty of Nations.* Wheaton, IL: Crossway, 2013. An analysis of economic systems and their effectiveness at creating wealth and alleviating poverty. One of the most thorough defenses of free market principles and biblical economic teachings.

Gwartney, James, Richard L. Stroup, and Dwight R. Lee. *Common Sense Economics: What Everyone Should Know about Wealth and Prosperity.* New York: St. Martin's Press, 2005. A basic primer on the fundamental elements, concepts, and components of economic systems. Written in a winsome tone for those without a background in economics regardless of religious beliefs or economic convictions.

Jones, David W., and Russell S. Woodbridge. *Health, Wealth & Happiness: Has the Prosperity Gospel Overshadowed the Gospel of Christ?* Grand Rapids: Kregel, 2011. A biblical and theological critique of the prosperity gospel, written for the church. In the second half of this volume the authors present constructive chapters and biblical teaching on suffering, wealth, poverty, and giving.

Keller, Timothy J. *Ministries of Mercy: The Call of the Jericho Road.* Phillipsburg, NJ: P & R, 1997. A biblical theology of the Christian duty to care for the poor. Half of the book consists of steps that could be taken by a church or other Christian organization to establish an effective ministry of mercy on the local level.

Lupton, Robert D. *Toxic Charity: How Churches and Charities Hurt Those They Help, and How to Reverse It.* New York: HarperOne, 2012. Written from a Christian perspective to a secular audience, this volume surveys the dangers of utilizing aid-based poverty relief models in contexts where developmental models are needed.

Nelson, Tom. *Work Matters: Connecting Sunday Worship to Monday Work.* Wheaton, IL: Crossway, 2011. A winsome theology of work and production written for the church. One of the most accessible volumes currently in print that addresses topic such as labor, vocation, and related subjects.

Olasky, Marvin. *The Tragedy of American Compassion.* New York: Regnery, 2004. A classic volume that presents a historical study showing how the burden of poverty relief was shifted from the church to the government within American society. Implicitly argues for a return to local, church-based poverty alleviation.

Richards, Jay W. *Money, Greed, and God: Why Capitalism Is the Solution and Not the Problem.* New York: HarperOne, 2009. Written from a Christian perspective to a secular audience, this volume seeks to debunk a number of myths related to free-market capitalism and presents a Judeo-Christian perspective on the economy and material goods.

Schneider, John R. *The Good of Affluence: Seeking God in a Culture of Wealth.* Grand Rapids: Eerdmans, 2002. Written in response to popular treatments of money and the economy that adopt a socialist perspective, this book seeks to show the inherent goodness of the material world and argues for a biblically-based, free-market, view of stewardship.

Old Testament

New Testament